Abusive Relationships

How to Get Rid of This Relationship

(Most Dangerous Subtle Form of Narcissism From Emotionally Abusive Relationships)

Branden Maynard

Published By **Kate Sanders**

Branden Maynard

All Rights Reserved

Abusive Relationships: How to Get Rid of This Relationship (Most Dangerous Subtle Form of Narcissism From Emotionally Abusive Relationships)

ISBN 978-1-7772308-5-2

No part of this guidebook shall be reproduced in any form without permission in writing from the publisher except in the case of brief quotations embodied in critical articles or reviews.

Legal & Disclaimer

The information contained in this book is not designed to replace or take the place of any form of medicine or professional medical advice. The information in this book has been provided for educational & entertainment purposes only.

The information contained in this book has been compiled from sources deemed reliable, and it is accurate to the best of the Author's knowledge; however, the Author cannot guarantee its accuracy and validity and cannot be held liable for any errors or omissions. Changes are periodically made to this book. You must consult your doctor or get professional medical advice before using any of the suggested remedies, techniques, or information in this book.

Upon using the information contained in this book, you agree to hold harmless the Author from and against any damages, costs, and expenses, including any legal fees potentially resulting from the application of any of the information provided by this guide. This disclaimer applies to any damages or injury caused by the use and application, whether directly or indirectly, of any advice or information presented, whether for breach of contract, tort, negligence, personal injury, criminal intent, or under any other cause of action.

You agree to accept all risks of using the information presented inside this book. You need to consult a professional medical practitioner in order to ensure you are both able and healthy enough to participate in this program.

Table Of Contents

Chapter 1: The Concept Of Toxicity In Relationships 1

Chapter 2: Recognizing Toxicity 31

Chapter 3: The Impact Of Toxicity On Our Mental Health 38

Chapter 4: Dealing With Toxic People 41

Chapter 5: Moving Forward And Thriving 59

Chapter 6: Identifying Emotional Abuse. 68

Chapter 7: Types Of Emotional Abusers. 80

Chapter 8: The Science Behind Manipulation 93

Chapter 9: Personal Experiences And Narratives 103

Chapter 10: Emotional Hooks And Vulnerabilities 113

Chapter 11: Effective Counter-Techniques 125

Chapter 12: Embracing Self-Care And Healing.. 133

Chapter 13: Digital Age And Emotional Abuse... 143

Chapter 14: Emotional Abuse In Different Settings... 155

Chapter 15: Interactive Tools And Techniques... 165

Chapter 16: Creating Boundaries And Safe Spaces.. 177

Chapter 1: The Concept Of Toxicity In Relationships

Toxicity in relationships refers to styles of behavior which can be risky, detrimental, and emotionally draining for one or each events concerned. These behaviors can variety from passive-aggressive comments and belittling, to physical abuse and manipulation. The term "toxic" is used to offer an reason for the ones behaviors because of the fact, like a poison, they are capable of slowly erode the health and fitness of these involved, leaving them feeling depleted, hopeless, and trapped.

Recognizing toxicity in a courting is often hard due to the fact it could take location in many one-of-a-type bureaucracy. It isn't constantly smooth to look the caution signs and symptoms and signs and symptoms, in particular at the identical time as one is deeply invested within the dating. However, there are sure behaviors and styles that can be purple flags for toxicity. Toxicity in relationships can take many brilliant workplace paintings and may be difficult to understand, in particular if it has come to be normalized through the years.

The following are some commonplace traits of a poisonous courting:

1. Lack of appreciate: A poisonous courting is characterised through a loss of recognize among the occasions worried. This can arise in masses of fantastic techniques, which includes belittling, condescension, or dismissiveness.

Lack of admire is a not unusual characteristic of poisonous relationships. It can be exhibited in many splendid approaches, which incorporates:

a. Belittling: One associate can also moreover use insults or positioned-downs to make the opportunity person experience inferior. For example, they may make a laugh in their companion's look, intelligence, or competencies.

b. Condescension: A toxic partner may additionally speak proper right down to their associate or treat them like they will be an awful lot less realistic or succesful than they absolutely are. This should make the opportunity man or woman enjoy small and inadequate.

c. Dismissiveness: A poisonous accomplice won't take their associate's thoughts, feelings, or opinions appreciably. They can also push aside their problems or belittle them for expressing themselves.

d. Ignoring obstacles: A poisonous companion can also moreover brush aside their accomplice's barriers and do topics that they've explicitly stated they will be uncomfortable with. For example, they may pressure their partner into having sex or invade their privateness by way of way of going via their smartphone or laptop.

e. Withholding affection: A toxic accomplice may additionally use affection as a praise for extraordinary behavior or withhold it as a shape of punishment. This can make the other man or woman enjoy like they will be constantly on foot on eggshells.

Examples of lack of admire in a toxic relationship can be visible in:

John continuously belittles his partner, Sarah, through telling her she's now not as clever as him and that she can't do something proper.

Karen talks all the manner all the way down to her accomplice, Tom, and treats him like he's a little one. She tells him he is not capable of making important alternatives and that he goals her to manual him.

Mark dismisses his partner, Jane's, emotions and tells her she's overreacting while she expresses her problems approximately their relationship.

David ignores his accomplice, Lisa's, boundaries and pressures her into having sex even when she has explicitly stated she's now not inside the temper.

Rachel withholds affection from her partner, Alex, as a punishment while he would possibly no longer do what she desires or disagrees together with her critiques.

All of these behaviors can erode the honor and recall amongst companions and make the possibility individual feel small, unheard, and unimportant. If you are experiencing loss of apprehend in your relationship, it's miles critical to cope with the problem with your accomplice and are seeking out manual from a trusted friend or mental health professional.

2. Control and manipulation: A poisonous partner also can attempt to manage or

manage their partner's mind, emotions, and behaviors. This can encompass emotional blackmail, gaslighting, or making threats.

Control and manipulation are common functions of toxic relationships. A toxic accomplice may additionally moreover furthermore try to exert control over their companion's thoughts, feelings, and behaviors in masses of one-of-a-kind techniques. Here are some examples of methods this may occur:

a. Emotional blackmail: A poisonous associate can also furthermore use emotional blackmail to manipulate their associate's behavior. For example, they may threaten to move away if their accomplice does not do what they need or make their associate feel guilty for no longer complying with their wishes.

b. Gaslighting: This is a form of emotional abuse wherein a poisonous associate makes their partner query their very own reality. They may deny some element that befell or make their partner experience like they may be loopy for wondering or feeling a certain manner.

c.   Making threats: A toxic associate might also moreover moreover make threats to manipulate their partner's behavior. For instance, they may threaten to damage themselves or their associate if their companion does no longer do what they want.

d.   Excessive jealousy: A poisonous partner can also additionally moreover feel threatened through the usage of their partner's relationships with others and attempt to control who they talk to or spend time with. They can also moreover accuse their accomplice of cheating or emerge as irritated if their partner does no longer devote all in their interest to them.

e.   Isolating their accomplice: A toxic accomplice may additionally additionally moreover isolate their associate from their pals and own family to exert manipulate over them. They can also discourage their associate from spending time with others or cause them to experience answerable for trying to carry out that.

Examples of manipulate and manipulation in a poisonous dating may be seen in:

Sarah's associate, John, makes use of emotional blackmail to control her conduct. He threatens to go away her if she could not do what he wishes and makes her experience responsible for now not complying along with his needs.

Tom's accomplice, Karen, gaslights him by means of the use of denying subjects that came about or making him experience like he is loopy for questioning or feeling a excessive pleasant way.

Mark makes threats to manipulate his partner, Jane's, behavior. He threatens to damage her or himself if she does no longer do what he goals.

David is excessively jealous of his associate, Lisa's, relationships with others. He tries to control who she talks to and spends time with, and accuses her of dishonest.

Rachel isolates her associate, Alex, from his pals and family. She discourages him from spending time with others and makes him revel in guilty for seeking to do so.

All of those behaviors may additionally have vital outcomes for the companion being managed and manipulated. They can bring about feelings of anxiety, melancholy, low arrogance, and a sense of isolation. If you're experiencing manage or manipulation in your relationship, it is critical to are searching out help and help from a depended on buddy, member of the family, or intellectual fitness expert.

3. Inequality: In a toxic relationship, one companion can also have greater electricity or control than the alternative. This can bring about emotions of resentment, anger, and frustration.

Inequality is every special function of poisonous relationships, in which one companion has greater strength or manage than the opportunity. This can arise in masses of different strategies, which consist of:

a. Financial control: A poisonous partner may also control the rate range inside the dating, leaving the opportunity associate feeling financially established and powerless.

b. Decision-making: A toxic companion can also make all of the alternatives in the dating, leaving the alternative accomplice feeling unheard and unimportant.

c. Physical manage: A toxic companion may also moreover manipulate the physical region within the courting, which incorporates the bed room or the living room, leaving the alternative associate feeling uncomfortable and constrained.

d. Intellectual manipulate: A poisonous associate can also furthermore manipulate the highbrow area in the courting, which encompass what subjects are stated, what evaluations are right, and what ideals are allowed, leaving the opportunity companion feeling like they can not specific themselves freely.

Examples of inequality in a poisonous courting can be seen in:

Anna's associate, Mike, controls the rate range in the relationship, leaving Anna feeling financially based totally and powerless.

James' partner, Sarah, makes all of the selections within the dating, leaving James feeling unheard and unimportant.

Lisa's accomplice, Tim, controls the physical location within the relationship, together with the bedroom or the residing room, leaving Lisa feeling uncomfortable and restrained.

Matt's associate, Jen, controls the intellectual area in the courting, dictating what topics are noted, what critiques are relevant, and what beliefs are allowed, leaving Matt feeling like he can't specific himself freely.

Inequality in a courting can motive emotions of resentment, anger, and frustration, and may motive extended-term damage to the relationship. If you are experiencing inequality on your dating, it's far important to talk up and talk your feelings on your partner. If your companion is unwilling to trade, it is able to be crucial to are searching for help from a therapist or counselor to paintings through the ones issues.

4. Verbal and emotional abuse: Verbal and emotional abuse can take many one-of-a-kind office work, from yelling and call-calling to silent remedy and manipulation.

Verbal and emotional abuse are not unusual functions of poisonous relationships, and may take many one-of-a-type paperwork, at the facet of:

a. Yelling and make contact with-calling: A toxic accomplice may also additionally yell or scream at their accomplice, the use of derogatory language or insults to harm them emotionally.

b.   Silent treatment: A poisonous partner can also moreover use silence as a weapon, refusing to speak to their acccmplice for prolonged durations of time, leaving them feeling isolated and rejected.

c.   Gaslighting: A poisonous partner may also manage their companion's belief of fact, making them doubt their very own mind and emotions, and leaving them feeling harassed and disoriented.

d.   Criticism: A toxic accomplice may also moreover criticize their accomplice constantly, placing forward flaws and shortcomings, and leaving them feeling inadequate and nugatory.

Examples of verbal and emotional abuse in a poisonous relationship can be seen in:

Jake's companion, Samantha, constantly yells and curses at him, using derogatory language to harm him emotionally.

Emily's associate, David, uses the silent remedy whenever they have got an trouble, leaving Emily feeling remoted and rejected.

Mark's partner, Rachel, constantly criticizes him, citing his flaws and shortcomings, and leaving him feeling inadequate and worthless.

Nicole's companion, Tom, frequently makes use of gaslighting to manipulate her perception of truth, leaving her feeling careworn and disoriented.

Verbal and emotional abuse may be exceptionally detrimental to a person's highbrow health and shallowness, and may have extended-lasting results on their relationships and sizeable properly-being. If you are experiencing verbal or emotional abuse on your relationship, it's far crucial to looking for assist from a depended on buddy, family member, or therapist.

five. Isolation: A poisonous partner also can try to isolate their associate from buddies and own family, making them enjoy by myself and relying at the toxic accomplice for the whole thing.

Isolation is each exceptional characteristic of toxic relationships in which one partner also can try and isolate the opposite from buddies and family, making them revel in on my own and depending at the poisonous companion for the whole thing. This can display up in masses of particular strategies, on the side of:

a. Restricting conversation: A toxic companion can also limit their partner's functionality to talk with pals and own family individuals, collectively with monitoring their telephone or laptop utilization, or limiting their get proper of entry to to social media.

b. Discouraging social sports: A poisonous accomplice may additionally moreover discourage their companion from collaborating in social sports, together with going out with buddies or attending own family sports, leaving them feeling remoted and on my own.

c. Creating dependence: A poisonous accomplice may additionally create a feel of dependence thru presenting their companion with the whole thing they need, together with food, secure haven, and cash, whilst at the equal time proscribing their get right of access to to unique belongings of guide.

d. Manipulating the narrative: A toxic accomplice also can control the narrative throughout the courting to their associate's friends and family people, making it difficult for the associate to attain out for assist or guide.

Examples of isolation in a poisonous courting can be seen in:

Jason's partner, Amanda, restricts his capability to talk alongside along together with his pals and own family, tracking his phone and pc utilization.

Lily's companion, Alex, discourages her from attending social sports activities activities along with her buddies, leaving her feeling isolated and alone.

Sam's associate, Emily, creates a feel of dependence with the useful resource of the usage of supplying him with the whole thing he dreams, which incorporates food and safe haven, at the identical time as on the same time restricting his get right of access to to special property of help.

Mike's partner, Rachel, manipulates the narrative throughout the relationship, making it tough for him to attain out for assist or manual from his buddies and family.

Isolation in a courting may have intense consequences for a person's highbrow health and properly-being, and might make it difficult for them to leave the poisonous relationship. If you're experiencing isolation to your dating, it is crucial to gain out to relied on pals and circle of relatives humans for assist, and to are searching for assist from a therapist or counselor to paintings thru the ones troubles.

6. Lack of agree with: Trust is an vital element of any healthful dating. In a poisonous relationship, however, agree with is often absent or eroded over time.

Lack of trust is a common feature of poisonous relationships, wherein one or both partners may also additionally battle to accept as true with each extraordinary. This can appear in lots of various procedures, which encompass:

a. Jealousy: A poisonous partner may additionally end up jealous without issue, accusing their companion of infidelity with none proof.

b. Betrayal: A poisonous partner may also have betrayed their partner's take delivery of as real with within the beyond, making it hard for the companion to do not forget them all over again.

c. Lies: A poisonous companion can also furthermore lie frequently, making it tough for their companion to actually accept as genuine with them and to recognize what is proper.

d. Control: A toxic partner may try and manipulate their partner's conduct or restrict their freedom, that could result in a breakdown in take transport of as real with over time.

Examples of a lack of accept as actual with in a poisonous relationship can be seen in:

Sarah's associate, Michael, becomes jealous without trouble, accusing her of cheating without any proof.

Tom's accomplice, Jane, has betrayed his take delivery of as authentic with in the past, making it tough for him to just accept as real along with her all over again.

Chris's companion, David, lies often, making it difficult for Chris to just accept as proper with him and to realise what is actual.

Rachel's companion, John, attempts to control her behavior and restrict her freedom, which has brought about a breakdown in accept as proper with over the years.

A lack of take into account can be a big barrier to a healthy dating, and may reason large emotional pain and misery for every partners. If you are experiencing a loss of agree with in your dating, it is critical to talk brazenly alongside side your associate and to are searching out help from a therapist or counselor to art work via the ones issues.

7.   Physical abuse: Physical abuse is using physical strain to manipulate or harm another person. It can embody hitting, kicking, slapping, or other styles of violence.

Physical abuse is a important form of toxicity in a dating, in which one accomplice makes use of physical pressure to govern or harm the opportunity. This can take vicinity in lots of unique techniques, which include:

a.   Hitting or slapping: A toxic companion may also moreover use bodily strain to hit or slap their companion, inflicting physical damage and pain.

b. Kicking or pushing: A toxic associate can also moreover use bodily pressure to kick or push their associate, causing damage or harm.

c. Choking or strangling: A poisonous companion also can use bodily strain to choke or strangle their partner, which can be existence-threatening.

d. Use of guns: A poisonous accomplice also can use weapons or objects to threaten or damage their partner, that may purpose large emotional trauma.

Examples of bodily abuse in a poisonous relationship may be seen in:

James hits his accomplice, Lisa, whilst he gets indignant, inflicting bruises and injuries.

Samantha's companion, Mark, kicks her in some unspecified time in the future of arguments, leaving bruises and causing physical ache.

Carlos chokes his accomplice, Maria, in the course of fights, leaving her feeling scared and helpless.

David threatens his associate, Karen, with a knife within the route of arguments, inflicting terrific emotional trauma and distress.

Physical abuse is a severe shape of toxicity in a relationship and can motive huge harm and trauma to the victim. If you are experiencing physical abuse for your relationship, it's far important to are seeking out assist and aid from a therapist, counselor, or home violence hotline. Remember that you aren't by myself, and there are those who assist you to break out from an abusive situation.

eight. Jealousy: A poisonous accomplice may also additionally additionally grow to be jealous or possessive, accusing their companion of dishonest or being unfaithful with none proof to aid their claims.

Jealousy is a not unusual function of toxic relationships, wherein one accomplice can also moreover furthermore become overly possessive and suspicious of the opportunity's behavior. This can show up in many unique strategies, together with:

a. Accusations of infidelity: A toxic associate can also accuse their companion of dishonest or being unfaithful with none evidence to aid their claims.

b. Controlling conduct: A poisonous associate also can try to manipulate their accomplice's behavior, limiting their freedom and independence.

c. Monitoring cellphone calls and social media: A poisonous companion may additionally additionally display their accomplice's phone calls, messages, and social media hobby to keep tabs on their whereabouts and interactions with others.

d. Isolation from buddies and own family: A poisonous associate may also try to isolate their accomplice from friends and own family, making them more depending at the toxic companion for emotional guide.

Examples of jealousy in a poisonous courting can be seen in:

Tom's accomplice, Jane, becomes jealous and possessive, accusing him of cheating without any evidence to guide her claims.

Sarah's associate, Michael, attempts to manipulate her behavior and limit her freedom, turning into irritated even as she spends time with friends or circle of relatives.

Chris's accomplice, David, video show units his telephone calls and messages, turning into suspicious while he interacts with specific humans.

Rachel's partner, John, tries to isolate her from friends and own family, making her experience greater depending on him for emotional guide.

Jealousy can be a massive supply of hysteria and warfare in a courting, and can motive enormous emotional misery for each companions. If you're experiencing jealousy on your courting, it is vital to talk brazenly together along with your partner and to are trying to find for help from a therapist or counselor to paintings through these troubles.

Recognizing those tendencies can be tough, specifically if you are deeply invested inside the relationship. However, there are sure caution signs and symptoms and signs that permit you to apprehend at the same time as a dating is poisonous. These encompass:

Feeling tired: If you find out yourself feeling tired, depleted, or emotionally exhausted after spending time collectively together with your accomplice, this could be a sign that the connection is toxic.

Constant battle: If the connection is characterized through steady struggle, arguing, or stopping, that is a red flag for toxicity.

Feeling unheard: If your accomplice constantly ignores or dismisses your feelings or troubles, that is a signal of toxicity.

Feeling controlled: If you experience like your accomplice is trying to control or manage you, this is any other warning sign.

Feeling remoted: If your companion is maintaining apart you out of your buddies and own family, that is a signal of a toxic relationship.

If you apprehend those caution symptoms for your courting, it's miles crucial to perform that to shield yourself and heal. This can encompass putting obstacles, attempting to find useful aid from pals or a therapist, and, if crucial, leaving the relationship. Recognizing and handling toxicity in a dating is a difficult and emotional device, but it's miles crucial for accomplishing lengthy-time period fitness and happiness.

Recognizing the ones warning symptoms is an essential first step in managing toxicity in a courting. However, it is important to word that toxic conduct is frequently cyclical and may be tough to break loose from. If you discover your self in a poisonous dating, there are several steps you could take to shield yourself and heal:

1. Set boundaries

Clearly talk your wishes and expectations for your companion. Let them understand what behaviors aren't applicable, and stay with those barriers.

Setting boundaries is a essential step in creating a healthy and respectful dating. Here are a few suggestions for placing barriers together along with your associate:

i. Identify your desires: Before you can set boundaries together collectively together with your accomplice, you need to become aware about what your desires are. Think about what behaviors make you experience uncomfortable, disrespected, or risky.

ii.   Communicate your needs: Once you've got got diagnosed your desires, communicate them honestly and assertively to your partner. Use "I" statements to particular the way you sense and keep away from blaming or criticizing your accomplice.

iii.   Be ordinary: It's important to be steady in imposing your barriers. If your partner keeps to head your boundaries, calmly remind them of your expectations and the outcomes of no longer respecting them.

iv.   Seek help: If you're having problem putting and implementing barriers, are looking for help from a therapist or counselor. They will permit you to expand powerful communique skills and assertiveness strategies.

Examples of placing boundaries together with your companion consist of:

Letting your associate understand that it isn't always best for them to belittle or push aside your feelings and feelings.

Telling your accomplice that you need location and time for your self and that it's far vital for them to respect your barriers.

Letting your accomplice understand that you are not cushty with them tracking your cellular phone calls, messages, or social media interest.

Telling your companion that bodily violence or abuse isn't right and that you may not tolerate it to your dating.

By setting easy barriers and implementing them, you could create a greater healthy and additional respectful relationship along facet your partner. Remember which you need to be handled with admire and dignity, and placing boundaries is an vital step in accomplishing that.

2. Seek assist

Talk to depended on pals or family people approximately what you are going through. Consider looking for the help of a therapist or counselor who can offer extra assist and steering.

Chapter 2: Recognizing Toxicity

Signs and behaviors of toxic human beings

Different types of poisonous relationships and environments

Understanding the effect of toxicity on our mental fitness and fitness

Toxic partners can showcase quite a number symptoms and behaviors which can have terrible outcomes on their companions and relationships. Here are some common symptoms and symptoms and signs and symptoms and signs and symptoms and behaviors of toxic partners:

1. Jealousy and possessiveness: Toxic companions may grow to be excessively jealous or possessive, that may bring about controlling conduct. They may additionally try to restriction their associate's interactions with others, display their activities or accuse them of infidelity without evidence.

2. Manipulation: Manipulation is a common tactic used by toxic companions to govern their companions. They can also use guilt, threats, or emotional blackmail to get their manner, and may use their associate's vulnerabilities in the direction of them.

3. Verbal abuse: Verbal abuse can take many office paintings, such as insults, name-calling, and belittling. Toxic companions can also moreover furthermore use those strategies to undermine their accomplice's vanity and make them revel in inferior.

4. Emotional unavailability: Toxic partners can be emotionally unavailable, that could make it tough for their companion to sense emotionally linked to them. They can also additionally moreover keep away from emotional discussions or near down while their partner expresses their feelings.

five. Gaslighting: Gaslighting is a manipulative tactic wherein the toxic accomplice attempts to make their companion doubt their personal reality. They also can deny or distort statistics, blame their companion for topics that aren't their fault, or make their partner experience loopy or paranoid.

6. Controlling conduct: Toxic partners might also additionally moreover try and manipulate their companion's actions or picks, frequently below the guise of "shielding" or "looking after" them. They may moreover moreover make alternatives for his or her companion without consulting them, or

attempt to manipulate their accomplice's price range or social existence.

7. Lack of empathy: Toxic partners may be no longer capable or unwilling to empathize with their associate's emotions or dreams. They may moreover push aside their companion's issues, decrease their feelings, or be unresponsive to

Different sorts of toxic relationships and environments

Toxic relationships and environments are poor to as a minimum one's intellectual and physical well-being. They can purpose despair, anxiety, and other terrible psychological consequences. In this evaluation, we are able to find out the wonderful styles of toxic relationships and environments and their results on humans.

1. Emotional Abuse: Emotional abuse is a shape of poisonous dating wherein one companion uses phrases and actions to govern, manage, and demean the possibility.

This can encompass verbal insults, threats, and gaslighting, it truly is a way wherein the abuser attempts to steer the victim that they're loopy or imagining topics. Emotional abuse can go away sufferers feeling powerless, depressed, and worrying.

2. Physical Abuse: Physical abuse is a sort of poisonous relationship in which one companion makes use of physical stress to control and intimidate the alternative. This can encompass hitting, slapping, punching, and exclusive styles of physical violence. Physical abuse can go away sufferers with bodily injuries and emotional scars that would remaining a whole lifestyles.

3. Sexual Abuse: Sexual abuse is a sort of toxic dating where one companion makes use of sex as a method of manage and power over the opposite. This can encompass undesirable sexual advances, rape, and sexual coercion. Sexual abuse can leave sufferers feeling violated, powerless, and traumatized.

four. Narcissistic Abuse: Narcissistic abuse is a form of toxic courting wherein one associate uses their inflated feel of self-worth to govern and manage the opposite. This can embody gaslighting, emotional abuse, and withholding love and affection. Narcissistic abuse can depart sufferers feeling unworthy, harassed, and emotionally worn-out.

5. Co-dependency: Co-dependency is a form of poisonous dating in which one companion is overly relying at the possibility. This can embody sacrificing one's very personal wishes and desires for the sake of the opportunity, and allowing the alternative's terrible conduct. Co-dependency can leave sufferers feeling trapped and powerless.

6. Enmeshment: Enmeshment is a shape of poisonous courting in which one accomplice is overly involved inside the different's life. This can encompass controlling behavior, emotional manipulation, and emotional enmeshment, in which the

associate's feelings are carefully tied to the other's. Enmeshment can go away patients feeling suffocated and trapped.

7. Neglect: Neglect is a type of toxic surroundings in which one partner fails to provide the vital care and interest to the other. This can encompass neglecting emotional dreams, physical desires, and easy necessities which consist of meals and refuge. Neglect can go away sufferers feeling unimportant and unnoticed.

8. Addiction: Addiction is a shape of toxic surroundings wherein one or each partners are addicted to capsules, alcohol, or one-of-a-kind substances. This can bring about forget, abuse, and different horrible behaviors that might harm the connection and the human beings involved.

In prevent, toxic relationships and environments can have severe terrible effects on humans. It is important to understand the signs of toxicity and are attempting to find help if critical. Therapy and counseling can be useful for human beings who have professional toxic relationships or environments.

Chapter 3: The Impact Of Toxicity On Our Mental Health

Toxicity refers to any substance, relationship, or surroundings that has poor effects on our mental health and well-being. Toxicity can take area in various office work which includes abuse, neglect, trauma, and pressure, and can motive severa highbrow fitness issues.

1. Anxiety: Toxic environments can reason anxiety troubles, which may be characterised thru immoderate fear and worry. Individuals in poisonous environments can also additionally moreover experience constantly on aspect, with racing mind, coronary coronary coronary heart palpitations, and panic assaults. Toxic relationships can also purpose social anxiety, wherein human beings can also additionally become afraid of judgment or lousy interactions.

2. Depression: Toxic environments can cause depression, that is a mood sickness characterised by using persistent feelings of unhappiness, hopelessness, and worthlessness. Individuals in toxic environments might also moreover feel beaten and exhausted, with a loss of motivation and interest in sports they as quickly as loved.

three. Post-traumatic pressure sickness (PTSD): Exposure to poisonous environments which incorporates abuse or trauma can motive PTSD. Symptoms of PTSD consist of intrusive memories, nightmares, flashbacks, avoidance of triggers, and hypervigilance. Individuals with PTSD can also have difficulty slumbering, concentrating, and functioning in their each day lives.

four. Substance abuse: Toxic environments can growth the risk of substance abuse, wherein humans can also moreover turn to capsules or alcohol to cope with their awful emotions and recollections. Substance abuse can purpose addiction, impaired judgment, and bodily health issues.

Chapter 4: Dealing With Toxic People

Setting boundaries and setting ahead oneself

Communication techniques for handling poisonous human beings

Coping mechanisms for handling toxic interactions

Dealing with toxic people may be hard, but it is vital to defend your highbrow health and properly-being. Here are a few techniques for managing toxic people:

1. Setting obstacles and putting forward oneself: It is essential to set clean boundaries

with toxic human beings and talk them assertively. Boundaries can be bodily, emotional, and verbal, and they help defend your space and energy. For instance, you may say, "I don't experience cushty speaking about this topic," or "I need a few on my own time right now." It is important to be company and constant in imposing your boundaries.

2. Communication techniques for managing toxic humans: When speakme with poisonous humans, it's far critical to live calm and assertive. Use "I" statements to unique your emotions and desires, and keep away from blaming or criticizing the opportunity person. Listen actively to the possibility individual's mindset and try to find not unusual ground. It is likewise helpful to workout energetic listening and replicate decrease lower back what the alternative person is saying to expose that you understand.

three. Coping mechanisms for dealing with toxic interactions: Coping mechanisms can help you control your emotions and reactions on the same time as coping with poisonous people. Some powerful coping mechanisms consist of:

Deep respiratory and meditation: These techniques can help you calm your thoughts and decrease strain and tension.

Exercise: Physical pastime allow you to release pent-up emotions and beautify your mood.

Self-care: Prioritize self-care sports sports that help you sense snug and rejuvenated, inclusive of taking a heat tub, analyzing a e-book, or operating in the direction of yoga.

Seeking aid: Reach out to relied on friends, circle of relatives members, or intellectual fitness specialists for emotional aid and steerage.

It is vital to undergo in mind which you can't manipulate different humans's conduct, but you may manage your response to it. By setting barriers, talking assertively, and the use of effective coping mechanisms, you could manipulate toxic interactions and defend your intellectual fitness and well-being.

HEALING FROM TOXICITY

Understanding the healing technique and one-of-a-kind techniques to recovery

Self-care practices to guide recuperation

Coping with trauma and PTSD from toxic evaluations

Healing is a multifaceted gadget that consists of addressing the physical, emotional, and mental additives of an character's properly-being. The recuperation manner can variety relying on the sort of trauma or harm skilled, but it commonly consists of the following degrees:

1. Acknowledgment: The first step in the recovery approach is acknowledging the trauma or damage and its effect on your life.

This entails dealing with your emotions, thoughts, and emotions head-on, and accepting that recovery will take time.

2. Expression: Once you have got were given stated the trauma or damage, it's miles essential to specific your emotions and thoughts. This can contain talking to a therapist, writing in a magazine, or accomplishing modern expression which includes art or tune.

three. Processing: Processing consists of statistics the trauma or damage and its impact on your lifestyles. This consists of reflecting on your studies, identifying styles and triggers, and growing coping mechanisms to govern your emotions and reactions.

4. Acceptance: Acceptance entails coming to phrases with the trauma or damage and its impact on your life. This includes acknowledging that the trauma or harm has modified you, but it does not outline you. It moreover consists of growing a revel in of

forgiveness and compassion for yourself and others.

five. Integration: Integration entails incorporating the training found out from the recovery method into your each day life. This includes growing wholesome conduct, placing limitations, and keeping a satisfactory outlook on existence.

There are numerous techniques to recovery, each with its precise advantages and challenges. Here are some not unusual techniques:

1. Cognitive-behavioral therapy (CBT): Cognitive-behavioral treatment (CBT) is a type of psychotherapy that may be useful for humans who have professional trauma or damage. CBT focuses on figuring out and converting negative idea styles and behaviors that make contributions to emotional misery.

Here are a few methods that CBT may be useful for trauma or damage recovery:

a) Identifying horrible mind: CBT can help human beings emerge as aware of and venture awful mind that can be contributing to their emotional misery. For example, someone who changed into in a car twist of fate can also have horrible thoughts together with "I'm now not stable" or "I cannot take delivery of as actual with anyone.' CBT can help them task those mind and update them with greater sensible and quality ones.

b) Developing coping techniques: CBT can assist people growth coping mechanisms to manipulate their emotions and reactions to trauma or harm. These coping strategies can also include deep breathing, progressive muscle rest, or visualization strategies.

c) Exposure remedy: Exposure remedy is a form of CBT that includes progressively exposing human beings to the subjects that trigger their worrying recollections or fears. For instance, someone who have end up in a car twist of future may match with their therapist to regularly monitor themselves to using or being a passenger in a car.

d) Behavioral activation: CBT can assist people increase fantastic behaviors which could enhance their temper and well-being. This might also encompass scheduling exciting sports activities or spending time with loved ones.

e) CBT is a primarily based and purpose-orientated remedy that can be effective in assisting people recover from trauma or harm. It can be used on its own or in aggregate with unique treatment plans or treatments, together with medicinal drug or manual agencies

2. Eye Movement Desensitization and Reprocessing (EMDR): Eye Movement Desensitization and Reprocessing (EMDR) is a form of therapy that has been located to be effective in treating trauma, which include publish-disturbing pressure illness (PTSD). EMDR entails a therapist guiding the character thru a chain of eye moves or unique

sorts of bilateral stimulation on the identical time as they interest on demanding recollections, mind, or feelings.

Here are some methods that EMDR can be useful for trauma restoration:

a) Reducing the intensity of worrying recollections: EMDR can assist people approach disturbing memories in a way that reduces their emotional intensity. This may want to make the reminiscences experience an lousy lot much less overwhelming and decrease the misery associated with them.

b) Developing more healthy coping mechanisms: EMDR can assist people growth more healthy coping mechanisms to cope with worrying reminiscences and their related signs. This can embody developing new strategies of considering the trauma, growing relaxation strategies, or mastering a way to manipulate tension or specific hard feelings.

c) Improving vanity: EMDR can assist people make bigger a extra great experience of self and increase their vanity. This can be especially beneficial for people who have professional trauma that has left them feeling helpless or powerless.

d) Enhancing commonplace nicely-being: EMDR has been decided to be powerful in enhancing wellknown properly-being, which incorporates reducing signs and signs and symptoms of hysteria and despair, improving sleep, and growing emotions of happiness and contentment.

EMDR is a particularly new remedy that has received reputation in modern-day years for its effectiveness in treating trauma. While it is able to not be appropriate for anybody, it may be a treasured device for individuals who are suffering to triumph over worrying studies

3. Mindfulness-based totally absolutely remedy plans: Mindfulness-primarily based absolutely remedy alternatives are a hard and fast of treatments that assist individuals to end up more conscious and present inside the second. These healing procedures train

individuals to reputation on the winning 2d, to emerge as privy to their mind and emotions, and to practice self-compassion. Mindfulness-primarily based remedy plans can embody:

i. Mindfulness-primarily based completely sincerely strain cut charge (MBSR): MBSR is a program that combines mindfulness meditation, body attention, and yoga to help people control stress and enhance ordinary nicely-being. The utility is usually eight weeks lengthy and includes weekly instructions and every day mindfulness meditation exercise.

ii. Mindfulness-primarily based completely cognitive therapy (MBCT): MBCT is a therapy that combines mindfulness meditation with cognitive-behavioral remedy (CBT) to help humans control horrific thoughts and emotions. MBCT has been confirmed to be powerful in treating despair and anxiety.

iii. Acceptance and self-discipline treatment (ACT): ACT is a shape of remedy that allows people discover ways to take delivery of their thoughts and feelings, in preference to in search of to manage or avoid them. ACT teaches humans to interest on their values and take movement in keeping with those values, even within the face of tough thoughts and feelings.

four. Medication: Medication may be a useful remedy preference for humans experiencing symptoms of despair, anxiety, and outstanding highbrow health conditions related to trauma or harm. However, it's far vital to have a look at that medicine should in no manner be used because the handiest treatment method, and ought to continuously be used along aspect remedy and specific recovery techniques.

Medications typically used to deal with intellectual fitness situations encompass antidepressants, anti-tension medicinal capsules, and mood stabilizers. These medicinal tablets work with the useful resource of changing the stages of nice chemical materials inside the mind, along with serotonin and dopamine, which have an impact on temper and conduct.

It's crucial to work carefully with a healthcare expert, including a psychiatrist or a number one care health practitioner, to determine if remedy is the right treatment method to your specific wishes. They let you understand the potential benefits and risks of taking medicinal drug, and can display your development to make sure that the drugs is strolling successfully.

It's furthermore important to phrase that remedy should have side outcomes, and that it could make an effort to locate the proper treatment and dosage that works exceptional for you. Patience, staying strength, and verbal exchange along side your healthcare expert are key to finding the proper remedy plan to your dreams.

5. Alternative treatment plans: Alternative recuperation tactics along with acupuncture, at the aspect of acupuncture, yoga, and meditation, can be useful in managing strain and promoting relaxation. These restoration procedures can also help humans expand a greater enjoy of self-consciousness and inner peace, which can be specially beneficial for those who have professional trauma or damage.

Acupuncture, for example, entails the insertion of skinny needles into unique elements on the body to sell healing and stability. This remedy has been set up to be powerful in reducing stress and anxiety, similarly to enhancing sleep and fundamental well-being.

Yoga is a bodily and intellectual exercise that includes a mixture of respiratory carrying activities, meditation, and bodily postures. Practicing yoga can help humans enlarge more flexibility, energy, and stability, at the identical time as furthermore lowering strain and selling rest.

Meditation includes the workout of quieting the thoughts and specializing within the winning 2d. This can be completed through numerous techniques, along with mindfulness meditation, which includes listening to the winning 2d without judgment. Meditation has been showed to be powerful in decreasing stress, anxiety, and despair, in addition to improving basic nicely-being.

It's crucial to study that opportunity treatment plans have to be used at the side of, rather than as an possibility for, conventional treatments including psychotherapy and medicine. Working with a healthcare professional or licensed practitioner can help ensure that those remedies are constant and powerful on your unique dreams.

In stop, the recovery gadget is a complex and multifaceted journey that consists of acknowledging, expressing, processing, accepting, and integrating demanding reviews. There are numerous methods to healing, which consist of CBT, EMDR, mindfulness-based totally totally remedies, treatment, and opportunity recovery strategies. It is vital to artwork with a highbrow fitness professional to boom an individualized technique to recuperation that meets your precise dreams and desires.

Self-care practices to assist recovery

Self-care practices are critical to useful resource healing, in particular for people who have expert trauma or harm. Self-care practices comprise taking deliberate moves to take care of one's physical, emotional, and highbrow properly-being. Here are some self-care practices that can guide recovery:

1. Prioritize sleep: Getting sufficient sleep is critical for normal health and properly-being. It also can help enhance temper, lessen pressure, and sell recovery. Aim for at the least seven to 8 hours of sleep each night time.

2. Engage in bodily hobby: Exercise can help lessen strain, beautify temper, and promote bodily fitness. Find physical sports activities sports that you experience, which incorporates on foot, swimming, or yoga.

3. Eat a balanced weight loss plan: Eating a balanced healthy dietweight-reduction plan that consists of quit result, greens, whole grains, and lean protein can provide vital vitamins to resource physical and intellectual fitness.

four. Practice relaxation strategies: Relaxation strategies such as deep respiratory, meditation, or yoga can help lessen strain and sell a experience of calm.

five. Set limitations: Setting barriers is critical to guard your physical, emotional, and intellectual nicely-being. Learn to mention "no" whilst you want to, and prioritize your very very own wishes and dreams.

6. Engage in pastimes and pursuits: Engaging in hobbies and hobbies can provide

a sense of success and delight. Find sports sports which you enjoy, together with analyzing, portray, or being attentive to track.

7. Connect with others: Building and retaining healthy relationships can provide emotional help and help lessen emotions of isolation. Reach out to friends and own family individuals, or recall becoming a member of a manual organization.

Chapter 5: Moving Forward And Thriving

Rebuilding consider and relationships after toxicity

Strategies for growing wholesome relationships and environments

Finding which means and motive past toxic reviews

Rebuilding accept as real with and relationships after experiencing toxicity can be a hard and complicated approach. Toxic relationships can motive large damage to recall and might bring about a breakdown in conversation, feelings of betrayal, and harm. However, with time, effort, and patience, it's miles feasible to rebuild preserve in thoughts and repair relationships. Here are some techniques that could help rebuild recall and relationships after toxicity:

1. Take responsibility: If you've got performed a role inside the toxic courting, take responsibility to your moves and widely known the damage that you have triggered. This can help rebuild take transport of as real with and display a dedication to change.

2. Apologize: Apologize virtually and take obligation in your actions. Be unique approximately what you are sorry for and the way you need to make amends.

3. Communicate efficiently: Communication is crucial to rebuilding agree with and relationships. Practice energetic listening, percent your mind and feelings, and be open to feedback.

four. Establish boundaries: Establishing easy limitations can help save you future toxicity and provide a experience of protection and protection. Work together to set limitations that understand every other's desires and goals.

5. Practice forgiveness: Forgiveness is a crucial part of rebuilding consider and relationsnips. It includes letting pass of past hurts and shifting beforehand with a self-discipline to repair and rebuild the relationship.

6. Seek expert assist: If rebuilding be given as authentic with and relationships feels difficult, undergo in thoughts running with a therapist or counselor who makes a speciality of relationships. A professional can assist navigate the manner and provide help and steerage.

7. Take time to heal: Healing from the results of a toxic courting takes time. Allow your self and the opportunity man or woman time to technique their emotions and

emotions, and be patient as you figure to rebuild do not forget and relationships.

In quit, rebuilding accept as authentic with and relationships after experiencing toxicity can be tough, however it is possible. Taking responsibility, apologizing, talking efficiently, putting in limitations, education forgiveness, looking for expert help, and taking time to heal are all techniques that can help rebuild trust and restore relationships. Remember, rebuilding take transport of as right with and relationships takes time, strive, and staying power, however with dedication and backbone, it's miles viable to create wholesome and suitable relationships.

Strategies for growing healthful relationships and environments

Developing healthy relationships and environments is critical to our mental fitness and nicely-being. Healthy relationships and environments are characterised with the resource of manner of accept as true with, understand, powerful verbal exchange, and a experience of safety and security. Here are some techniques for growing healthful relationships and environments:

1. Practice lively listening: Active listening consists of listening to the speaker, summarizing their words, and clarifying any misunderstandings. This can assist assemble believe and foster powerful verbal exchange.

2. Communicate successfully: Effective verbal exchange involves expressing your thoughts and emotions in a clean and respectful way. Use "I" statements to explicit the way you sense and avoid blame or criticism.

three. Set boundaries: Setting obstacles is important to maintaining healthy relationships and environments. Establish clean barriers that understand each extraordinary's desires and dreams and speak them successfully.

4. Practice empathy: Empathy consists of know-how and acknowledging the emotions

and studies of others. Practice putting yourself in excellent people's shoes and show knowledge and compassion.

five. Build bear in mind: Trust is important to wholesome relationships and environments. Build take transport of as real with by using way of being sincere, reliable, and constant for your movements.

6. Foster a enjoy of protection and protection: A revel in of safety and safety is important to healthy relationships and environments. Create a solid and supportive environment through way of respecting every different's limitations, emotions, and stories.

7. Practice forgiveness: Forgiveness is vital to preserving healthful relationships and environments. Practice letting pass of beyond hurts and shifting earlier with a willpower to restore and rebuild the connection.

eight. Seek professional help: If growing healthy relationships and environments feels hard, don't forget jogging with a therapist or counselor who focuses on relationships. A professional can assist navigate the method and provide assist and steerage.

In cease, developing healthful relationships and environments takes strive and commitment, however it's far important to our intellectual health and properly-being. Practice active listening, communicate successfully, set limitations, practice empathy, construct trust, foster a enjoy of protection and safety, workout forgiveness, and are searching for professional help if vital. By following those strategies, we're capable of increase healthy relationships and environments that promote our widely widespread well-being and happiness.

Finding that means and motive beyond toxic reviews

Finding which means that and purpose past toxic reviews may be a tough and complex way. Toxic research can go away us feeling damage, disillusioned, and unsure approximately our future. However, with time, attempt, and self-mirrored image, it's far viable to find out which means and reason beyond toxicity. Here are some techniques which can assist find out which means and purpose past toxic research:

1. Practice self-reflected photo: Self-reflected photo consists of searching inward and analyzing our thoughts, feelings, and behaviors. Reflect for your values, strengths, and weaknesses, and remember how the ones can help guide your destiny alternatives.

2. Seek manual: Seeking manual from loved ones, pals, or a therapist can offer a enjoy of consolation and validation. Surround your self with individuals who resource and inspire you.

3. Explore new pursuits: Exploring new hobbies and pastimes can help amplify your mind-set and provide a enjoy of motive. Consider trying new sports activities activities, joining a club, or volunteering.

4. Set dreams: Setting desires can assist offer direction and attention. Identify quick-time period and lengthy-time period desires and create a plan to collect them.

five. Find this means that in beyond memories: Finding due to this in beyond testimonies can assist provide a experience of closure and information. Consider how beyond reviews have common you and the way they are able to help guide your future options.

6. Practice gratitude: Practicing gratitude entails spotting and appreciating the wonderful things to your existence. Focus on the powerful components of your existence and exercise expressing gratitude on a each day basis.

7. Embrace trade: Embracing change may be hard, however it can additionally provide new possibilities for growth and improvement. Be open to new reviews and don't forget how they will be capable of assist form your destiny.

In quit, locating which means and purpose past poisonous studies takes time, attempt, and self-reflected photo. Practice self-mirrored image, are searching for help, discover new hobbies, set dreams, find out that means in beyond recollections, exercise gratitude, and embody exchange. By following these strategies, it's far feasible to find that means and motive beyond toxicity and create a satisfying and practical lifestyles. Remember, the restoration machine takes time, but with staying strength and resolution, it is possible to transport forward and create a brighter destiny.

Chapter 6: Identifying Emotional Abuse

In the superb tapestry of human interactions, emotional abuse frequently stays a subtle, nearly imperceptible thread. Yet, its presence can overshadow and warp the most intimate of relationships, leaving at the back of a direction of confusion, harm, and self-doubt. Identifying emotional abuse is the primary, important step towards restoration and empowerment. This bankruptcy interests to shed moderate on the nuanced markers of such abuse, guiding readers to decide the subtle from the overt, the occasional misstep from the chronic manipulative patterns. Together, we will adventure into the middle of abusive dynamics, equipping ourselves with the information and notion required to understand, venture, and ultimately ruin free from the ones negative styles. Let's embark in this critical exploration, for in information lies the critical factor to liberation.

Subtle Signs and Red Flags

The landscape of emotional abuse is dotted with signs and symptoms and symptoms— some obvious, even as others are greater elusive, nearly whispered. It's the diffused symptoms and symptoms, those that gently tug at one's instinct, that may be the maximum volatile. Their very subtleness guarantees they frequently cross ignored, disregarded as overreactions or disregarded as remoted incidents. Yet, these may be the very harbingers of deeper, more insidious manipulation patterns.

1. Casual Disregard: Ever felt that your feelings, mind, or opinions have been frequently minimized or outright dismissed? This may take vicinity as playful teasing that constantly seems to move a line, or in the form of comments that reduce your achievements, making them appear insignificant.

2. Boundary Violations: A friend who again and again borrows cash without returning, a accomplice who insists on gaining access to your personal messages, or a member of the family who desires excessive time without thinking about your desires—the ones are all signs and symptoms of a crucial disrespect for boundaries.

three. Guilt Tripping: "After all I've achieved for you!" or "You're so egocentric for trying this!" Such statements motive to result in guilt, making the sufferer feel indebted or inside the incorrect for putting forward their desires or rights.

4. Constant Criticism: While high-quality feedback is critical for boom, a continuous circulate of terrible feedback, in particular the ones focused on one's man or woman or personality, can erode self esteem.

5. Gaslighting: Named after a traditional movie in which a husband tries to make his spouse accept as true with she's losing her mind, gaslighting consists of denying statistics, distorting realities, or trivializing the sufferer's feelings. Over time, sufferers begin doubting their memory, perception, or perhaps sanity.

6. Silent Treatment: Using silence as a weapon, the abuser manipulates thru withholding affection, communique, or interest, forcing the sufferer to experience demanding, eager to assuage, or even desperate.

7. Over-dependence or Hyper-autonomy: The abuser might also additionally each mission themselves as overly established, portray themselves because the helpless sufferer looking regular care, or they will take the alternative direction, showcasing immoderate autonomy to the point in which the sufferer's characteristic or importance of their lifestyles is totally faded.

Recognizing those diffused symptoms and signs and symptoms and signs and symptoms calls for astute commentary, self-pondered picture, and frequently, being attentive to that intestine feeling that insists, "Something isn't proper." These signs and signs and symptoms are the pink flags, signaling that the relationship is veering off into unstable territory.

Beyond the Obvious: Unraveling Covert Abuse

While overt emotional abuse—shouting, blatant grievance, direct humiliation—is discernible, covert emotional abuse is the silent, murky undercurrent that draws its electricity from being inconspicuous. This shape of abuse is insidious, frequently going ignored even by using the sufferer for extended durations.

1. Ambiguity: Covert abusers enjoy ambiguity. They would probably deliver backhanded compliments or make statements which could have dual meanings—one innocent and the opposite, derogatory.

2. Withheld Affection: Rather than outright rejecting or criticizing, a covert abuser would possibly in all likelihood withhold affection or appreciation, especially as quickly as they're aware about it's miles most favored, the usage of it as a device to control and manipulate.

3. Passive Aggressiveness: Instead of direct struggle of phrases, the abuser accommodations to sulking, subtle digs, or movements that they comprehend will dissatisfied the sufferer, excellent to later deny any terrible purpose.

4. Feigned Helplessness: The "I can not live with out you" or "You're the high-quality appropriate issue in my life" strains, while used manipulatively, can lure sufferers in a cycle of responsibility.

five. Triangulation: The abuser introduces the opinion or stance of some other individual (frequently fictional) to validate their non-public factor of view or to pit the sufferer in opposition to this 0.33 celebration. It's a tactic to create lack of self guarantee and confusion.

6. Projected Blame: The abuser is forever the victim, always moving blame for his or her movements onto occasions or, more often, onto the actual victim. Any try to hold them responsible is met with deflection.

7. Strategic Absence: Unlike the silent remedy, it's far a right away reaction to a perceived moderate, strategic absence includes the abuser distancing themselves at important moments to create tension and lack of confidence.

eight. Financial Manipulation: Covertly controlling rate range, making big monetary choices without session, or passive resistance to monetary discussions are all methods the abuser ensures dominance.

Diving deep into the shadows of covert abuse is similar to navigating a maze—it calls for discernment, staying power, and resilience. But shining a mild on the ones shadows, understanding their nooks and corners, is step one inside the course of liberation.

Both diffused signs and symptoms and symptoms and symptoms and covert abuse patterns intertwine to create a web that can ensnare the unsuspecting. But statistics is electricity. By recognizing the ones styles and knowledge their dynamics, you may reclaim their narrative, their self confidence, and in the long run, their lifestyles. The adventure in advance will unveil greater layers, extra strategies, and extra desire

Case Studies: Real-life Instances

The actual effect and nature of emotional abuse can regularly be first-class understood thru actual-life debts. These case research offer a glimpse into the lives of these who've professional such trauma and spotlight the sorts of abusive behavior.

Case Study 1: Maya and the Gaslighting Partner

Maya, a vivacious woman in her late twenties, started courting Alex, whom she met via a mutual pal. In the preliminary months, their relationship turned into image-perfect. However, as time advanced, Alex's behavior have become regarding. Whenever Maya confronted him about discrepancies in his tales, he may additionally twist the narrative, making her doubt her reminiscence. For instance, after canceling a date, he may want to later insist he had informed her, even though he hadn't. Maya began 2d-guessing herself, often feeling disoriented. It wasn't till a therapist added her to the term "gaslighting" that she recognized Alex's manipulations.

Case Study 2: Raj and the Controlling Friend

Raj modified into constantly the peacemaker in his group of friends. But his bond with Sam became in contrast to every one-of-a-kind. They shared secrets and strategies, dreams, and lots of recollections. However, Sam had a dependancy of making picks for Raj—in which that they had consume, which movies that they had watch, even influencing Raj's profession picks. Whenever Raj confirmed independence, Sam may sulk or hotel to passive-aggressive jibes. The friendship took a toll on Raj's self-esteem, making him sense he could not make alternatives without Sam's approval.

Case Study 3: Eleanor and the Silent Mother

Growing up, Eleanor continuously strived to benefit her mom's approval. But each time she carried out something, her mom may also withhold affection. She in no manner shouted or criticized Eleanor right now. Instead, she'd withdraw, sometimes no longer speaking to Eleanor for days. Eleanor grew up demanding, continuously tiptoeing round her mom, frightened of displeasing her. The silent treatments have been her mom's manner of keeping control.

Case Study four: Diego and the Financially Manipulative Spouse

Diego, a software program application engineer, married Lisa, a agreement creator. Soon after, Lisa started making big financial alternatives without consulting Diego—like shopping expensive devices or making an investment large sums of coins. When Diego attempted to talk approximately rate range, Lisa would both save you the communique or play the victim, accusing Diego of no longer trusting her. Diego felt trapped, as confronting Lisa induced more chaos, however staying silent supposed relinquishing manage over their charge range.

Case Study 5: Aisha and the Projected Blame at Work

Aisha loved her way as a crew leader in a reputed agency. However, her supervisor, Neil, have emerge as a everyday supply of strain. Whenever there had been mistakes in tasks, despite the fact that they have been now not Aisha's fault, Neil would insinuate that she have become responsible. He'd often say such things as, "If you had handiest managed your group higher." Aisha decided herself all the time at the protecting, even though she knew she wasn't at fault.

Each of those case studies underscores the numerous faces of emotional abuse. From private relationships to professional settings, manipulative behaviors can take vicinity in myriad ways. Recognizing them is the first step within the route of empowerment and breaking loose.

Chapter 7: Types Of Emotional Abusers

Understanding emotional abuse requires a deep dive into the minds of folks who perpetrate it. At the center of many abusive behaviors are positive personality sorts with super dispositions and styles. In this bankruptcy, we are capable of demystify three such personalities often linked with emotionally abusive inclinations: narcissists, sociopaths, and psychopaths. By greedy the intricacies in their behaviors, we are able to better arm ourselves in the course in their strategies.

Narcissists: The Ego-Centric Controllers

Narcissism stems from Greek mythology in which Narcissus, captivated by way of using the use of his reflection, stared at it till he changed right into a flower. While a diploma of narcissism is wholesome and vital for shallowness, pathological narcissism can be poor.

1. Definition: A narcissist has an inflated revel in of self-importance, a deep want for

admiration, and a loss of empathy for others. Their self esteem is usually unstable, resting on the shaky grounds of external validation.

2. Key Traits:

Grandiosity: They take delivery of as proper with they may be precise and unique, deserving of specific interest.

Validation Seeking: Compliments fuel them, while criticism, actual or perceived, is met with hostility.

Manipulation: They use others as tools for validation, often discarding them after they surrender to be of use.

3. Emotional Abuse Patterns:

Gaslighting: Making the sufferer doubt their truth to maintain manipulate.

Love-bombing: Showering immoderate affection first of all, first-rate to withdraw it as punishment later.

Triangulation: Pitting people in competition to every special to live the middle of interest.

Sociopaths: The Unanchored Drifters

While frequently used interchangeably with psychopathy, sociopathy has splendid tendencies. Rooted in a unmarried's surroundings or demanding beyond, it's far lots much less approximately innate tendencies and further about superior behaviors.

1. Definition: Sociopathy is a character illness characterized with the useful resource of persistent delinquent conduct, impaired empathy and remorse, and bold, disinhibited, egotistical traits.

2. Key Traits:

Impulsiveness: They act with out considering effects, main to a course of chaos.

Deceitfulness: Lying or manipulating for personal advantage or delight is commonplace.

Recklessness: Disregard for the protection of themselves or others.

Aggression: Physical or verbal aggression, often without provocation.

3. Emotional Abuse Patterns:

Charm and Manipulation: Using aura to govern after which make the maximum.

Inconsistency: Their testimonies, behaviors, and emotions alternate unpredictably.

Absence of Guilt: They not often, if ever, sense guilt for their movements, making repeated offenses probably.

Psychopaths: The Cold Calculators

Intriguing and chilling, the area of a psychopath is one in all calculated moves, without emotional depth. While all psychopaths may not be criminals, their loss of empathy makes them functionality threats in intimate settings.

1. Definition: Psychopathy is a character disorder characterised with the aid of chronic delinquent conduct, faded empathy and remorse, and bold, disinhibited behavior. It's greater innate than sociopathy, frequently related to physiological variations in the brain.

2. Key Traits:

Superficial Charm: They are often articulate and can be captivating, but it's a masks for manipulation.

Emotional Vacuity: They do not form real emotional connections, viewing people as mere device.

Calculated Risks: Unlike the impulsiveness of a sociopath, a psychopath's movements are coldly calculated.

Fearlessness: They have a immoderate threshold for risk and don't worry results as most do.

three. Emotional Abuse Patterns:

Predatory Behavior: They find out a sufferer's weak point and take advantage of it methodically.

Control: Dominating every component of the victim's lifestyles, regularly the usage of intimidation.

Isolation: Cutting the victim off from help systems to ensure dependency.

Distinguishing Among The Three:

While there are overlaps, discerning amongst those personalities is important:

Origins: Narcissism is about inflated ego, sociopathy is rooted in surroundings, and psychopathy in biology.

Emotional Depth: Narcissists can sense harm (particularly to their ego), sociopaths can shape attachments (regardless of the fact that shallow), and psychopaths live largely indifferent.

Impulsiveness vs. Calculation: Sociopaths are extra impulsive; psychopaths are coldly calculated. Narcissists can swing between every, based mostly on what feeds their ego.

Gaslighters and Their Tactics

Gaslighting, a form of highbrow manipulation, seeks to sow seeds of doubt in someone, making them query their memory, notion, or sanity. The term originates from the 1944 film "Gaslight," in which a husband manipulates his partner into believing she's losing her thoughts. This chapter delves into the area of gaslighters, uncovering their strategies to equip readers with the expertise needed to apprehend and counteract this form of emotional abuse.

Profile of a Gaslighter

Before diving into their techniques, it is essential to recognize the gaslighter's psyche:

Need for Control: Central to a gaslighter's conduct is their choice for manage and energy over each different individual.

Defensiveness: They may possibly lodge to gaslighting at the same time as faced approximately their conduct to prevent obligation.

Lack of Empathy: Gaslighters regularly can not or do no longer need to apprehend others' emotions or perspectives.

Insecurity: Deep down, many gaslighters are insecure, using manipulation as a protection mechanism.

Common Tactics Employed through Gaslighters

1. Trivializing Feelings: Gaslighters restriction the emotions and reactions of their sufferers. Comments like "You're too touchy" or "You're overreacting" are not unusual, aiming to make the sufferer doubt the validity in their feelings.

2. Denying Reality: One of the primary techniques is outright denial. Even if the sufferer has evidence of the gaslighter's wrongdoing, they'll face responses like, "That

in no manner came about" or "I in no way stated that."

three. Diverting the Blame: Rather than taking duty, gaslighters redirect the blame, making the sufferer enjoy responsible. "You made me do this" or "If you hadn't completed X, I might now not have performed Y" are conventional refrains.

four. Withholding Information: By keeping the victim within the dark or supplying partial records, gaslighters create an environment of uncertainty, making the sufferer depending on them for "truth."

5. Countering Memories: Gaslighters frequently mission the victim's reminiscence of occasions, pronouncing such things as, "You keep in mind subjects wrong all of the time" or "That's now not the way it befell."

6. Projecting: Gaslighters are adept at projecting their shortcomings onto their sufferers. A dishonest gaslighter might also

additionally accuse their partner of infidelity with none foundation.

7. Withdrawing or Stonewalling: By refusing to have interaction in a communication, gaslighters create a wall of silence, making patients doubt themselves and what they recognize to be real.

eight. Reinforcing Doubt: By praising the sufferer on occasion, gaslighters create a sense of dependency. This juxtaposition of grievance and espresso validation continues the sufferer off-balance and trying to find the gaslighter's approval.

Recognizing Gaslighting

Awareness is the primary line of defense in opposition to gaslighting. If you:

Frequently 2d-wager your memories or perceptions

Feel confused or crazy round a specific man or woman

Constantly make an apology, even while you accept as true with you haven't completed whatever incorrect

Feel a developing enjoy of self-doubt

You is probably a victim of gaslighting. Recognizing the signs and symptoms is the first step toward seeking out assist and countering those manipulative techniques.

Gaslighting, a covert form of emotional abuse, is corrosive, principal to a diminishing enjoy of self-worth in the victim. By expertise the gaslighter's techniques, you can construct resilience in opposition to this shape of manipulation and bypass toward recovery and self-empowerment.

The Spectrum of Toxicity

Human behaviors, specifically those categorised as poisonous, exist alongside a spectrum. Not each toxic behavior consists of the same weight or has the same effect. By conceptualizing toxicity on a spectrum, we are able to higher apprehend the nuances, evaluate our relationships more successfully, and determine on the wonderful path of movement.

Low-Level Toxicity

At this cuit of the spectrum, behaviors are regularly diffused and may be once in a while exhibited. These movements may be effortlessly neglected or excused, in particular if they will be rare.

1. Casual Negativity: These human beings could possibly often bitch, be cynical, or showcase pessimism, that may often drain the ones round them.

2. Passive Aggressiveness: Instead of confronting issues at once, they may use sarcasm, deliver silent remedies, or subtly undermine others.

three. Occasional Manipulation: They may moreover from time to time use emotional manipulation for minor personal income or advantages, however now not habitually.

Moderate Toxicity

Behaviors on this class are greater stated and ordinary. They are greater hard to push aside and might begin causing important strain in relationships.

1. Regular Manipulation: Using guilt, emotional blackmail, or deception becomes a greater common device to get what they need.

2. Verbal Abuse: This can comprise everyday instances of belittling, commonplace shouting, or consistent derogatory comments.

three. Blame-transferring: Individuals never take responsibility for their moves and generally shift the blame to others, heading off obligation.

Chapter 8: The Science Behind Manipulation

As humans, we're all liable to manipulation in a unmarried shape or some other. While some kinds of manipulation can be benign or even beneficial, together with a teacher motivating a scholar to attain their potential, there are darker, more insidious paperwork. This bankruptcy delves into the psychological underpinnings of manipulative conduct, losing mild on why a few people resort to such strategies and the way they effectively ensnare their sufferers.

Psychological Underpinnings of Abusive Behavior

1. Control and Power Dynamics:

At the coronary heart of manipulation lies the choice for manage. Abusers frequently experience empowered after they manage others, stemming from their non-public feelings of powerlessness or inadequacy. By manipulating others, they seize up on those feelings, growing a fake experience of superiority.

2. Insecure Attachment Styles:

Research indicates that human beings with insecure attachment styles, often developed in formative years because of inconsistent or unpredictable caregiving, would in all likelihood lodge to manipulative behaviors in relationships. These behaviors characteristic inaccurate tries to create safety or avoid abandonment.

three. Cognitive Dissonance:

Manipulators frequently face inner conflicts amongst their movements and ideals. To clear up this pain, they will convince themselves that their manipulative behaviors are justified or maybe benevolent, thereby decreasing the internal tension they sense.

4. Social Learning Theory:

Some manipulators undertake abusive behaviors after witnessing or experiencing them in the course of their young people. According to the social mastering principle, behaviors are determined out thru looking and imitating others, especially authoritative figures in a unmarried's existence.

5. Narcissism and Egocentrism:

Individuals with narcissistic trends regularly have an inflated experience of their private significance and a deep want for excessive hobby and admiration. This can purpose manipulative behaviors to hold their self-image and make sure that they stay at the middle of interest.

6. Fear of Vulnerability:

For some, manipulation is a safety mechanism to keep away from emotional vulnerability. By controlling and manipulating others, they prevent themselves from getting emotionally damage or feeling exposed.

7. Emotional Regulation Difficulties:

Some people have hassle handling their emotions, main them to externalize their feelings. They might likely use manipulation as a tool to sell off their emotional turmoil onto others, making sure they don't need to face or manner their feelings right away.

The Brain and Manipulation:

Modern neuroscience affords insights into how manipulators carry out at a neural stage:

Dopaminergic Reward Pathways: Manipulation and manage can stimulate the mind's praise centers, releasing dopamine, a neurotransmitter related to delight and reinforcement. This chemical release should make manipulation addictive for a few humans.

Reduced Empathy Regions: Studies have proven that people who display off manipulative or delinquent behaviors often have decreased hobby in mind regions associated with empathy, making it less complicated for them to damage others with out feeling remorse.

Heightened Stress Responses: Chronic manipulators may additionally additionally show off heightened stress responses, using them to govern their environment (along with humans) to mitigate emotions of anxiety.

In know-how the deep-rooted intellectual mechanisms that stress manipulative behaviors, we're higher organized to understand, confront, and defend ourselves from such moves. By shedding moderate at the origins and intricacies of manipulation, we can also foster empathy and help for the ones trapped in the cycle of manipulation, be it as a culprit or a victim, and are searching for for pathways to recuperation and know-how.

The Abuser's Perspective: What Drives Them?

It is often difficult for the ones who have been victimized to recognize the motivations at the back of their abuser's moves. Understanding the abuser's attitude isn't always about justifying or excusing their behavior, but instead gaining insights into the complex interaction of things that stress them to have interaction in manipulation and abuse. Here, we are going to delve into the thoughts-set and drivers of abusive people.

1. Deep-Seated Insecurity:

Many abusive people harbor profound feelings of loss of self assurance. They can also additionally have grown up feeling insufficient, unloved, or invalidated. By maintaining manage over a few other, they momentarily alleviate those emotions, growing a fake experience of self esteem and importance.

2. Past Trauma:

Traumatic stories, especially subsequently of childhood, can mildew an character's perceptions and behaviors. Those who expert abuse, forget about approximately about, or witnessed dysfunctional relationships may want to probable mirror those styles, believing them to be 'ordinary' or 'proper'.

three. Desire for Power and Control:

At the middle of most abusive behaviors is the innate choice to have power and manage over some other man or woman.

four. Fear of Abandonment:

Some abusers deeply worry abandonment, which might in all likelihood stem from beyond tales of being left, betrayed, or rejected. Their manipulative moves, paradoxically, are frequently tries to preserve the sufferer close to, making sure they won't face abandonment once more.

five. Lack of Empathy:

Empathy, the functionality to understand and percentage the emotions of a few unique, might be stunted in lots of abusers. This loss of empathy permits them to inflict ache without feeling real regret or facts the depth of their moves.

6. Sociocultural Influences:

In advantageous societies or communities, dominance and manage in relationships is probably normalized or even glorified. Abusers in such settings might also acquire as actual with that their moves aren't only suitable however also expected.

7. Cognitive Distortions:

Abusers frequently have interaction in distorted thinking patterns. They might likely justify their actions through rationalizations, limit the ache they reason, or usually blame the victim. These distortions protect them from confronting the fact of their conduct.

8. Emotional Dysregulation:

Some abusers struggle to control and adjust their emotions. When faced with emotional misery, they lash out, using abuse as a erroneous coping mechanism.

nine. Need for Validation:

Some abusers are on a perpetual quest for validation. They want normal confirmation of their nicely worth, and once they do now not get hold of it, they lodge to manipulation or abuse to extract it forcibly from their patients.

10. Fear of Intimacy:

While it might appear counterintuitive, a few abusers are deeply frightened of actual intimacy and connection. By retaining a facade of manage and power, they keep their sufferers at a distance, ensuring they don't want to stand the vulnerabilities that consist of real closeness.

Supported thru Academic Research and Studies

The realm of psychological abuse and manipulation isn't always just a be counted of private evaluations and anecdotes. Over the various years, full-size instructional studies and research have delved into the intricacies of abusive conduct, its origins, its results, and its functionality treatments. Grounding our facts in empirical proof lends credibility and depth to the hassle reachable. Let's discover the essential factor findings from renowned research on this area.

1. Attachment Theories and Abuse:

John Bowlby's Attachment Theory posits that our early memories with caregivers shape our attachment patterns, which effect our adult relationships. Studies have located a correlation among insecure attachment patterns (worrying and avoidant) and abusive behaviors in relationships.

Reference: Mikulincer, M., & Shaver, P. R. (2016). Attachment in adulthood: Structure, dynamics, and exchange. Guilford Publications.

Chapter 9: Personal Experiences And Narratives

The human spirit's resilience is evident at the same time as we delve into the harrowing but inspiring debts of survivors of emotional abuse. While educational studies offers a theoretical framework, those non-public narratives lend a voice to endless souls who've endured, resisted, and in the long run triumphed over their abusers. Let's embark on a adventure through some of the ones testimonies, data the nuances of their research and the facts they have got gleaned alongside the way.

1. Clara: The Invisible Chains

Clara grew up in a conservative family wherein voicing one's emotions come to be discouraged. Her accomplice, ten years her senior, regarded fascinating and protecting first of all. But quick, the protective veil slipped to show a manipulate freak. Clara recounts the endless instances she have become informed she changed into "overreacting" or "too sensitive" at the equal time as she voiced her discomfort. I started doubting my feelings, my recollections," she presentations. Eventually, remedy and a supportive buddy circle empowered her to interrupt free.

2. Raj: The Subtle Stranglehold

Raj's narrative is a powerful reminder that emotional abuse isn't restrained through gender or societal roles. His companion's everyday belittlement, her sly remarks befell as 'jokes', and her persistent refusal to famend his professional accomplishments wore down his conceitedness. "I felt like I grow to be continuously walking on eggshells, nerve-racking approximately triggering any other tirade," Raj admits. His turning factor became a workshop on emotional well-being, in which he diagnosed the toxic patterns and sought intervention.

three. Aisha: Love Doesn't Hurt

A passionate artist, Aisha's international revolved spherical her canvases and colors. Her companion, to begin with supportive, started out expressing disdain for her art work, calling it "childish" and "a waste of time". He isolated her from pals and subtly manipulated her into leaving at the back of her passion. A danger come across with a fellow artist reignited her spirit, and she determined out love want to no longer stifle; it need to encourage.

four. Leo: Breaking Generational Curses

Coming from a lineage of stoic men, Leo believed showing vulnerability was a sign of weak spot. His partner exploited this notion, the use of his insecurities towards him. "It have become a constant electricity play, in which I felt I continuously had to prove my nicely really well worth," he recalls. A own family counseling consultation uncovered the generational styles of emotional suppression and abuse, propelling Leo within the route of restoration and breaking the cycle.

5. Maya: Echoes of Childhood

Maya's story underscores how youngsters trauma can set the level for grownup relationships. Having grown up with an emotionally some distance flung mother, Maya have become interested in partners who contemplated that coldness. "It have become a familiar dance. The chase, the choice, and the eventual cold shoulder," she shows. A assist company for survivors of emotional abuse have turn out to be her sanctuary, in which she observed to rewrite her narrative.

These stories characteristic poignant reminders that emotional abuse manifests in myriad techniques. They additionally underscore the boundless resilience inherent in every survivor, and the way, with the right manual and popularity, you likely can reclaim their narrative and rebuild a existence full of dignity, recognize, and self-love.

Exploring Diverse Perspectives Across Age, Gender, and Cultures

Emotional abuse, as pervasive as it is, does no longer occur uniformly at some stage in awesome segments of society. It takes on severa hues and intensities relying on someone's age, gender, cultural ancient past, or even societal norms. By shining a highlight on numerous reviews, we intention to weave a holistic tapestry that captures the complexities of emotional abuse in its entirety.

1. Age Dynamics: From Young to Old

Adolescents and Young Adults: With the surge of social media and peer pressures, more youthful humans grapple with cyberbullying, peer manipulation, and romantic relationships that regularly skirt the traces of consent and admire. Jenny, a college freshman, shared, "The barrage of hurtful feedback on my posts made me query my properly well worth."

Midlife: As human beings navigate marriage, parenthood, and professional lives, emotional abuse can take place as electricity struggles, monetary manipulation, and parental alienation. Mark, a forty-3 hundred and sixty five days-vintage father, recalls, "My ex-associate subtly grew to grow to be our children towards me. It modified into coronary coronary heart-wrenching."

Elderly: Senior residents face unique demanding situations. From elder abuse via caregivers or own family members to societal forget about, emotional torment can be profound. As Mrs. Vasquez, a 70-12 months-vintage retiree, locations it, "Being dealt with as if you're invisible or a burden chips away at your soul."

2. Gendered Experiences: Beyond Binary Norms

Women: Historically, ladies for the duration of cultures have been subjected to patriarchal norms, managing emotional subjugation in various forms, from marital pressures to place of business harassment.

Men: Societal expectancies of stoicism and 'machismo' have to make guys silent sufferers, hesitant to voice their emotional struggles or are looking for assist.

Non-Binary and Transgender: This community faces a unique set of worrying situations, stopping societal prejudices, and intimate companion abuses that make the maximum their vulnerabilities. Alex, a non-binary individual, said, "Every slight or insult felt like an attack on my very identity."

three. Cultural Lenses: The Global Spectrum

Eastern Cultures: In many Asian societies, concepts like own family honor and filial piety can turn out to be gear for emotional manipulation. Ravi, from India, highlights, "I changed into coerced into a marriage for the sake of own family honor."

Western Cultures: Individualism and the pursuit of personal happiness may additionally deliver its set of stressful situations, like isolation, which can be exploited through manipulative companions or friends.

Indigenous Communities: Rooted in deep-seated traditions, indigenous cultures on occasion grapple with the juxtaposition of retaining customs and addressing ingrained emotional abuse patterns.

four. Intersections: When Categories Collide

Often, an character's enjoy with emotional abuse lies at the intersection of severa classes. A younger transgender woman of colour, for example, could possibly face compounded layers of emotional misery, given her age, gender identification, and racial historical beyond.

Recognizing the severa tactics emotional abuse manifests at some point of notable societal segments is vital. It emphasizes the want for tailored interventions and a multi-dimensional method in addressing and mitigating emotional abuse.

The Psychological Aftermath of Emotional Abuse

The echoes of emotional abuse can reverberate prolonged after the actual occasions have ceased. Emotional scars, in evaluation to bodily ones, are regularly invisible, making them even more insidious and tough to address. To actually hold near the profound effect of emotional maltreatment, we need to delve into the myriad intellectual outcomes survivors often grapple with.

1. Erosion of Self-properly well worth

Self-doubt: Constant belittlement, grievance, and humiliation can instill a profound enjoy of self-doubt in sufferers. Over time, they will internalize the ones horrible affirmations, thinking their competencies, selections, or maybe their perceptions of reality.

Low vanity: A continual revel in of worthlessness or feeling 'an entire lot much less than' can permeate each aspect of a survivor's existence, from expert endeavors to personal relationships.

2. Anxiety and Stress Disorders

Generalized Anxiety Disorder (GAD): Living below the shadow of unpredictability and worry can result in pervasive tension about severa elements of life, no longer absolutely the abusive situation.

Post-Traumatic Stress Disorder (PTSD): Flashbacks, nightmares, and excessive anxiety as a result of the demanding emotional abuse episodes can culminate in PTSD, a debilitating situation.

Chapter 10: Emotional Hooks And Vulnerabilities

Why we get involved

Emotional abuse, at the same time as universally poor, does not uniformly have an impact on honestly all of us. The complex net of manipulation is predicated carefully on tapping into the victim's emotional hooks and vulnerabilities. Recognizing and knowledge the ones emotional triggers is step one within the direction of empowerment and prevention. In this financial disaster, we delve deep into the psychology within the back of why we get ensnared within the toxic dance of emotional abuse and the manner our intrinsic vulnerabilities play a element.

1. The Need for Love and Affection

Humans, with the aid of manner of nature, are social creatures with an innate choice to attach, belong, and be cherished. Abusers can take gain of this important need thru:

Withholding Affection: By being unpredictable with their affection, abusers create an emotional seesaw. This continues the victim continuously looking for their validation and approval.

Love Bombing: In the initial levels, abusers could likely bathe the victim with immoderate affection, devices, and interest, growing a robust bond this is difficult to break.

2. Childhood Patterns and Conditioning

Our teenagers critiques extensively shape our person behaviors and relationships. Some vulnerabilities stem from:

Parental Dynamics: Growing up with emotionally unavailable or abusive dad and mom can normalize toxic behaviors for youngsters, making them extra inclined as adults.

Early Traumas: Experiences like bullying, neglect about, or early losses can create deep-seated vulnerabilities that abusers might possibly latch onto.

3. Fear of Abandonment

For many, the concern of being by myself or deserted a ways outweighs the ache of staying in a toxic courting. Abusers leverage this worry by way of way of:

Threatening to Leave: Regularly alluding to leaving or completing the connection can keep the victim in a perpetual nation of hysteria and appeasement.

Isolation: By placing apart patients from friends and circle of relatives, abusers motive them to greater based definitely, amplifying the priority of abandonment.

4. Low Self-virtually well well worth and Self-esteem

A dwindled revel in of self esteem ought to make individuals greater tolerant of mistreatment:

Internalizing Blame: Victims may additionally moreover consider they deserve the abuse or that it's far a end bring about their inadequacy.

Settling for Less: Believing they may be not worthy of actual love and recognize, they'll dangle to abusive relationships, thinking it's far the exceptional they are able to get.

five. Cognitive Dissonance

When our beliefs and actions conflict, it creates a psychological soreness known as cognitive dissonance. In the context of abuse:

Denial: Victims might in all likelihood deny the abuse or downplay its severity to reconcile their desire of staying with the conflicting fact of being mistreated.

Justifying the Abuser: They may want to in all likelihood rationalize the abuser's behavior, attributing it to stress, teenagers trauma, or other outdoor factors.

6. The Investment Theory

Over time, sufferers would possibly likely experience they've got invested an excessive amount of to go away:

Sunk Cost Fallacy: Believing they have got sacrificed an excessive amount of (time, feelings, assets), they live, hoping matters will decorate.

Future Hopes: Clinging to the nice recollections and the initial days of affection, they preserve onto the choice that the abuser will change.

It's essential to apprehend that those vulnerabilities are not weaknesses. They're intrinsic human desires and evaluations that abusers make the maximum. Recognizing them offers sufferers the readability and energy to disentangle themselves from the emotional quagmire and are searching for more healthful relationships.

Self-reputation: Recognizing Your Vulnerabilities

At the center of our emotional landscapes lies the complex matrix of our vulnerabilities. These smooth spots, derived from beyond reports, innate temperaments, and social conditioning, regularly pressure our picks, reactions, and relationships. While vulnerabilities are an essential a part of our human revel in, it's miles via self-awareness that we are able to avoid having them be our undoing. Here, we delve into the transformative journey of recognizing and know-how our vulnerabilities to foster greater healthy relationships and a robust experience of self.

1. Introspection: The Mirror to the Soul

To start facts our vulnerabilities, we want to first cultivate the addiction of introspection.

Journaling: Regularly jotting down your feelings, critiques, and triggers can provide precious insights into patterns that leave you prone.

Mindfulness and Meditation: These practices anchor us to the existing, helping in recognizing and accepting our emotional responses with cut judgment.

2. Unearth the Past

Our vulnerabilities often have deep-rooted origins, tied to past traumas, critiques, or upbringing.

Childhood Dynamics: Reflecting on your childhood, the nature of attachment with primary caregivers, and early reports can shed mild on many vulnerabilities.

Past Relationships: Identifying styles in beyond relationships, whether romantic, familial, or platonic, can help pinpoint triggers and easy spots.

three. Embrace Feedback

Sometimes, an outsider's attitude can provide clarity that introspection might possibly pass over.

Open Conversations: Engaging in sincere, open dialogues with trusted buddies or circle of relatives about perceived weaknesses can provide treasured insights.

Therapy: A expert can assist understand and deal with vulnerabilities in a established, supportive environment.

4. Recognizing Physical Manifestations

Our our bodies often react viscerally to emotional triggers.

Bodily Reactions: Noticing recurrent bodily signs and signs, like belly pain, palpitations, or a lump in the throat all through specific situations, can hint at underlying vulnerabilities.

Behavioral Patterns: Procrastination, defensiveness, or over-reimbursement may want to likely suggest regions of emotional ache or loss of self belief.

5. Challenge Cognitive Distortions

Our vulnerabilities can distort our perception of situations, vital to unwarranted fears or insecurities.

Reality Testing: Question your ideals and fears. Are they based totally mostly on facts or derived from vulnerabilities?

Positive Affirmations: Combat horrible self-talk and irrational fears with the beneficial resource of reinforcing excessive satisfactory beliefs approximately oneself.

6. Acceptance and Growth

Recognizing vulnerabilities is just the first step; acceptance is vital.

Self-compassion: Treat yourself with the identical kindness and records as you can a cherished one. Every man or woman has vulnerabilities; they do now not outline your sincerely clearly worth.

Empowerment Through Knowledge: Understanding your triggers equips you to navigate conditions better and set healthful barriers.

Embracing self-reputation could no longer without a doubt prevent others from exploiting our vulnerabilities; it paves the manner for actual self-boom, enriched relationships, and a existence led with authenticity and self belief.

Building Resilience Against Manipulation

Manipulation, in its many office work, is a device employed thru way of those looking for manage over others. It flourishes on exploiting vulnerabilities, bending perceptions, and tough boundaries. The maximum great protection in opposition to manipulation is resilience—a combination of self-attention, emotional intelligence, and firm barriers. In this phase, we are able to explore actionable strategies to cultivate resilience, making sure you still be steadfast and unyielding inside the face of manipulation.

1. Strengthening Emotional Intelligence (EI)

Emotional intelligence acts as a guard, alerting and protecting you from manipulation.

Self-recognition: Recognize and understand your emotions. By know-how your emotional triggers, you can prevent them from being exploited.

Empathy: Understand the feelings of others. This allows you to parent right feelings from manipulative strategies.

2. Educate Yourself on Manipulation Techniques

Knowledge is strength. Recognizing manipulation strategies makes them plenty less effective.

Gaslighting: Be aware of attempts to distort your reality or make you doubt your reminiscences.

Fear, Obligation, Guilt (FOG): These are powerful emotional drivers utilized in manipulation. Recognizing them can lessen their affect.

3. Establish and Maintain Boundaries

Clear barriers act as defensive boundaries closer to manipulation.

Express Your Limits: Clearly kingdom what you're cushty with and stand organisation for your alternatives.

Regularly Re-examine: Circumstances and feelings change. It's crucial to think another time and modify limitations as desired.

Chapter 11: Effective Counter-Techniques

Recognizing and Disengaging from Gaslighting

Gaslighting is a sinister form of manipulation wherein the abuser seeks to make the sufferer doubt their truth, memory, or sanity. The time period originates from the play and subsequent movie "Gas Light," wherein a husband tries to make his associate trust she's losing her mind. Recognizing and finally disengaging from this manipulative tactic is important for intellectual nicely-being and readability. Here's how:

Understanding the Signs of Gaslighting

To counteract gaslighting, one must first understand it.

Trivializing Feelings: Abusers could in all likelihood declare which you're overreacting or being too sensitive even as you unique issues.

Denial of Previous Actions: Even if a few problem came about currently, a gaslighter might possibly deny that it ever passed off.

Withholding Information: This would possibly seem as pretending now not to understand or refusing to concentrate.

Projecting Blame: Gaslighters frequently accuse the victim of the very behavior they are showing.

Strategies for Disengaging

Once you've got identified gaslighting, the following step is to disengage and defend your self.

Trust Your Memories and Feelings: Regular journaling can assist hold a clear report of events and interactions.

Avoid Justifying: When you're positive of your memories or emotions, avoid entering into a debate with the gaslighter. It regularly leads nowhere and high-quality motives more confusion.

Seek External Validation: Speak with depended on pals or family approximately your opinions to validate your feelings and reminiscences.

Limit Engagement: If secure to perform that, limit your interactions with the gaslighter. This may additionally mean setting limitations or maybe reducing ties.

Consider Professional Help: Therapy can provide techniques for managing gaslighting and support get hold of as actual with for your recollections and perceptions.

Gaslighting can be disorienting and deeply terrible. It's essential to recognize it for what it is: a tool of manipulate and manipulation. By understanding its signs and symptoms and the usage of strategies to disengage, you reclaim your reality, reminiscences, and sanity. Remember, you have to trust on your enjoy and feelings.

Creating Emotional Distance

Creating emotional distance is an crucial approach on the identical time as handling manipulative or toxic humans. It consists of setting apart your emotions and emotions from those imposed upon you via the alternative individual, due to this maintaining your highbrow nicely-being and experience of self. This does now not always advocate bodily separation; it's miles approximately constructing an inner barrier that allows you to interact without being deeply affected emotionally.

Why Emotional Distance is Important

Self-maintenance: Constant publicity to emotional manipulation can be draining. Distance permits defend you from capability damage.

Clarity of Thought: Emotional involvement can cloud judgment. Distance gives angle, thinking about more intention choice-making.

Maintaining Control: Emotional manipulators thrive on controlling reactions. By distancing yourself emotionally, you regain manage over your responses.

Strategies for Creating Emotional Distance

1. Mindfulness and Self-interest: Practicing mindfulness allow you to stay gift and apprehend whilst a person is trying to govern your emotions. Through self-awareness, you can pick out out your triggers and paintings inside the direction of neutralizing them.

2. Limit Exposure: If feasible, lessen the amount of time you spend with the individual or in situations which is probably emotionally draining.

three. Reframing Interactions: View interactions as if you're an observer, in preference to a participant. This can assist in detaching emotionally from the situation.

4. Boundaries: Set clean emotional and bodily boundaries. Inform the other character about those barriers, and be everyday in imposing them.

five. Seek Support: Engaging in conversations with relied on buddies or circle of relatives can offer validation and perspective. They can act as sounding boards, assisting you parent your emotions from those being imposed on you.

6. Professional Counseling: Therapists can provide coping mechanisms tailor-made to your particular scenario. They can also offer insights into why you may revel in deeply tied to the man or woman or scenario and manual you in putting in distance.

7. Practice Self-care: Engage in activities that assist rejuvenate you emotionally. This may be analyzing, meditation, exercise, or any interest that permits you loosen up and refocus.

eight. Affirmations: Remind yourself of your without a doubt really worth and the importance of your nicely-being. Positive affirmations can supply a lift on your need for distance and beautify your treatment.

9. Educate Yourself: Understand the techniques utilized by emotional manipulators. Recognizing those can assist in

preempting them and building emotional defenses.

By growing emotional distance, you prioritize your well-being over the chaos or negativity introduced with the aid of using manner of others. It's a form of self-care and self-admire, making sure that your emotions remain to your control. It's essential to endure in thoughts that distancing oneself emotionally may not equate to coldness or lack of compassion; it's far about ensuring emotional safety and intellectual fitness.

Assertiveness Techniques

Being assertive approach expressing one's thoughts, emotions, and dreams in an open, sincere, and respectful manner. It stands in evaluation to passive behavior (wherein one may want to no longer express their desires or feelings) and competitive conduct (in which one expresses their needs in a way that disregards others). For the ones entangled with manipulative humans, developing assertiveness is pivotal to set limitations and save you further emotional damage.

Why Assertiveness Matters

Voice and Validation: Assertiveness offers you a voice, allowing you to validate your feelings and perspectives.

Boundary Setting: It allows in developing and preserving personal limitations that shield your emotional and mental well-being.

Reduced Stress: Directly addressing problems reduces ambiguity and pressure that comes from unspoken tensions.

Relationship Enhancement: Open and clean conversation can bring about superior relationships, even out of doors of manipulative dynamics.

Chapter 12: Embracing Self-Care And Healing

Emotional trauma, especially on the equal time as prolonged, may additionally have lasting impacts on one's mental, emotional, and even bodily nicely-being. However, with the proper aid, belongings, and self-care practices, restoration isn't simplest a possibility—it is a promise. This financial ruin delves into the essentiality of self-care and guides you via the plethora of property available to expedite your adventure toward healing.

Mental Health Resources and Professional Help

The Importance of Seeking Help

No depend the intensity or the period of emotional abuse, it is important to recognize that searching out assist is not a signal of susceptible point. Instead, it's a testomony for your strength and determination to reclaim your life and your nicely-being.

1.   Therapy and Counseling: Engaging with a professional therapist or counselor can provide you with equipment and coping mechanisms to way trauma and assemble resilience.

Individual Therapy: A one-on-one installing which you may speak and dissect your critiques and feelings with a skilled therapist.

Group Therapy: Engaging with a group of people who've had comparable opinions. This putting can offer a feel of network and validation.

Cognitive Behavioral Therapy (CBT): This approach helps find out and alternate horrible perception patterns and behaviors.

2.   Psychiatric Help: Some people may also gain from medicine to govern signs and symptoms like anxiety or despair, often the aftermath of emotional abuse. Consultation with a psychiatrist is essential.

three. Helplines and Crisis Centers: These provide right now help, particularly at some point of moments of extreme distress. They can also guide you to more lengthy-time period aid.

4. Online Platforms: In the virtual age, severa on line structures offer assets, digital counseling, and supportive companies.

five. Books and Literature: Several self-assist books, studies papers, and autobiographical debts can provide insights, steering, and solace.

6. Workshops and Retreats: Dedicated to recovery from emotional trauma, the ones offer in depth remedy, meditation, and coping strategies.

Finding the Right Fit

Remember, truly everyone's adventure is precise. It's crucial to:

Research: Understand the therapist's or aid's method, credentials, and evaluations.

Trial: Sometimes, you might need to have interaction with a couple of therapists or assets to discover the proper healthy.

Trust your Gut: Your consolation is paramount. If a few element feels off or if you do now not resonate with a therapist or technique, it's far good enough to are looking for options.

Embracing Self-care

Self-care goes beyond spa days and relaxation—it is approximately constructing practices that nurture your thoughts, body, and soul.

1. Routine: Establishing a each day regular can provide a experience of normality and purpose.

2. Physical Activity: Whether it's miles yoga, taking walks, or good sized workout workout routines, physical interest can significantly decorate temper and reduce pressure.

3. Mindfulness and Meditation: These practices can decorate self-cognizance, reduce anxiety, and foster a deeper connection with oneself.

four. Healthy Eating: The food we eat can effect our mood and power. Focus on a balanced diet.

5. Journaling: Writing can be recuperation. It offers an outlet to express feelings and mirror for your recuperation adventure.

6. Art and Creativity: Engaging in inventive endeavors may be every recuperation and empowering.

7. Connect: Surround yourself with supportive buddies and own family. Social connections can extensively help in healing.

8. Limit Exposure: While healing, it is probably beneficial to limit exposure to triggers or poisonous people.

In end, healing from emotional trauma is a journey, not a holiday spot. Embrace the assets to be had and keep in mind—you aren't by myself. Embrace it, for every step you are taking is a step closer to a brighter, greater healthful destiny.

Therapeutic Practices: Meditation, Journaling, Therapy

In the aftermath of emotional misery or trauma, it's paramount to have avenues that facilitate inner peace, mirrored image, and recovery. Therapeutic practices like meditation, journaling, and remedy had been time-tested and are sponsored via severa research for their efficacy in assisting highbrow and emotional nicely-being. Let's delve deeper into each of those practices and recognize how they'll be seamlessly covered into one's restoration adventure.

Meditation

Meditation is a exercise that emphasizes mindfulness, recognition, and an prolonged recognition of the existing. It lets in humans to check their mind and feelings non-judgmentally, main to improved emotional law and reduced anxiety.

Benefits:

Reduces pressure and tension.

Enhances self-popularity.

Can enhance focus and focus.

Fosters a experience of calm and internal peace.

Getting Started:

Find a quiet vicinity.

Use guided meditations, to be had on numerous apps and net web sites, if you're new to the exercise.

Remember, it is right enough if your thoughts wanders; lightly deliver your recognition lower back.

Journaling

Journaling offers a stable and personal area to unique emotions, mind, and replicate upon evaluations. By placing pen to paper, you may gain clarity, validate emotions, and track restoration development.

Benefits:

Helps in processing emotions.

Can provide clarity in difficult situations.

Acts as a report of private growth and alternate.

Boosts memory and comprehension.

Getting Started:

Choose a medium that fits you: digital or conventional paper magazine.

Don't stress about structure; allow your mind flow.

Reflect on activates or questions in case you're unsure in which to start.

Therapy

Engaging with a professional therapist gives a established surroundings to apprehend, device, and cope with emotional misery. Therapists deliver professional insights, coping mechanisms, and provide a steady, non-judgmental location for discussions.

Benefits:

Professional guidance tailor-made to character goals.

Safe environment to speak approximately stressful memories.

Provides equipment and techniques for coping and healing.

Getting Started:

Research therapists based totally in your needs and their specialties.

Ensure they may be certified and function properly critiques or tips.

Schedule an initial session to determine if it is a superb healthy.

Incorporating those therapeutic practices into your everyday can be transformative. Each offers a very particular avenue for mirrored image, understanding, and boom. Embrace them at your non-public pace and in techniques that resonate with you. Remember, recuperation is a adventure, and people practices are gadget to beneficial aid you alongside the way.

Chapter 13: Digital Age And Emotional Abuse

The virtual age, characterized thru pervasive internet connectivity and the ubiquity of smartphones and exceptional gadgets, has revolutionized conversation and taken human beings nearer. However, with those upgrades come new avenues for emotional abuse. As our lives come to be an increasing number of intertwined with on-line structures, it's miles vital to recognize and combat the insidious varieties of emotional abuse that the virtual sphere can breed.

Identifying Online Gaslighting and Cyberbullying

The vastness of the net offers a platform for voices from anywhere within the globe. Yet, this same expansiveness can every so often guard people who desire to damage or control others. Two standard types of digital emotional abuse are on line gaslighting and cyberbullying.

Online Gaslighting

Gaslighting, a term originating from the 1944 movie "Gaslight," includes making a person doubt their fact. When translated to a web putting, gaslighting may appear to be:

Denial of Past Statements or Actions: An character may send hurtful messages after which deny doing so, likely even going as a long way as to control virtual proof.

Trolling: Deliberately making outrageous statements to confuse or damage others, then disregarding reactions as "over-sensitivity" or claiming it have become "most effective a funny tale."

Spreading False Information: Sharing deceptive or faux recollections about a person to harm their recognition or reason them to impeach their reality.

Invalidation: Dismissing a person's emotions or reactions to on line activities, claiming they're overreacting or too sensitive.

Cyberbullying

It can take vicinity in numerous techniques, together with:

Impersonation: Pretending to be someone else and acting in techniques to jeopardize their reputation.

Outing: Sharing a person's secrets and strategies or personal records with out consent.

Cyberstalking: Persistent on-line tracking, messaging, and harassment that induces worry.

Tackling the Issue

1. Education: Awareness is the first step. Understanding the signs and symptoms and signs and symptoms of on line gaslighting and cyberbullying empowers people to recognize and assignment abusive behavior.

2. Online Etiquette: Just as we train manners inside the real international, instilling a revel in of on line decorum is important. Kindness, respect, and empathy

want to be the cornerstones of on line interactions.

three. Privacy Measures: Using robust, unique passwords, often checking privateness settings, and being aware of shared content material can restrict risks.

4. Report and Block: Most on line systems have mechanisms to file abusive conduct. Utilizing those equipment can assist reduce down unwarranted actions.

5. Seek Support: Engage with relied on friends, family, or specialists even as encountering virtual emotional abuse.

In cease, the digital age, with all its marvels, brings with it worrying conditions that necessitate vigilance and versatility. By staying knowledgeable, looking for help, and fostering respectful on-line corporations, we are able to navigate the net global nicely and make certain that it remains a region for actual connection and increase.

Protecting Oneself within the Era of Social Media

Social media systems, from Instagram to Twitter, have become critical additives of our every day lives, allowing us to connect with pals, percentage lifestyles moments, and get right of access to worldwide information proper away. Being privy to these risks and records the manner to protect oneself can make sure that our social media revel in remains quality and secure.

Be Cautious with Personal Information

While it might be tempting to share every lifestyles occasion or success on social media, it's critical to be selective approximately what you put up. Avoid sharing overly non-public info like your own home deal with, workplace, or wonderful identifying information.

Adjust Privacy Settings

Regularly assessment and adjust the ones settings to govern who sees your posts and how your statistics is used. For example, you can set your account to non-public, making sure handiest legal fanatics can view your content cloth.

Be Skeptical of Unknown Contacts

While social media may be a first rate way to satisfy new humans, it's far critical to technique unknown contacts with caution. Avoid sharing non-public info with strangers and be skeptical of unsolicited messages or pal requests.

Limit Location Sharing

Many social media platforms offer talents that assist you to percentage your modern location. While this may be a laugh, it's miles frequently more consistent to keep away from the use of such abilties or to use them selectively.

Educate Yourself on Platform-specific Features

Each social media platform has its specific set of capabilities and capability dangers. Take the time to teach your self approximately the specific systems you operate. For example, recognize how tagging works on Facebook or how Stories feature on Instagram.

Don't Engage in Online Conflicts

It's smooth to get drawn into on-line debates or conflicts, mainly on systems like Twitter. However, those disputes can growth fast and result in undesirable hobby or even harassment. If you discover your self in a contentious scenario, it's far regularly excellent to disengage or block the opposite party.

Seek Support

If you ever experience overwhelmed or threatened via using something on social media, do not hesitate to are searching for help. This is probably inside the shape of friends, family, or even expert assist. They can offer steerage, attitude, and steps at the way to proceed.

In the ever-evolving landscape of social media, staying knowledgeable and vigilant is paramount. By taking a proactive approach for your on-line safety, you could revel in the numerous advantages of social media whilst minimizing functionality risks.

Case Studies: Online Manipulation Instances

The digital age, brimming with splendid interconnected networks, has sadly furthermore emerge as a playground for manipulators. Let's delve into some actual-life case research to shed mild on numerous on line manipulation strategies, the effects they've got on human beings, and classes we can examine from them.

1. Catfishing on a Dating App

Background: Sarah, a 28-365 days-vintage picture designer, started out out talking to "Mike," whom she met on a famous dating app. Mike claimed to be a 30-12 months-antique legal professional traveling often, which changed into why they couldn't meet in individual. Over several months, they built a sturdy emotional connection.

Manipulation: After some time, Mike commenced out having monetary problems on his journeys and started asking Sarah for small loans. Trusting Mike, Sarah lent him large sums. Eventually, Sarah had been given suspicious and did some investigating, most effective to discover "Mike" become sincerely "Carol," a 50-12 months-antique woman with a records of defrauding people.

Lesson: Always affirm the authenticity of individuals met on line, specially in the event that they keep away from face-to-face meetings. Be careful approximately lending cash based on take delivery of as proper with constructed sincerely thru online interactions.

2. Social Media Influencer Scandal

Background: Emily, a nicely-observed excursion influencer on Instagram, posted photos from her extravagant journeys, endorsing merchandise and promoting inn stays.

Manipulation: It have turn out to be later found out that lots of her adventure pictures were stock pics or taken from first rate vacationers. Additionally, products she claimed to like and use each day had been in reality props. Her fanatics were swayed thru manipulated content material, most critical them to buy products and services primarily based mostly on deceit.

Lesson: Always circulate-check facts and reviews from more than one assets in advance than making buy choices primarily based totally on influencer endorsements.

three. The "Viral" Misinformation Campaign

Background: During a great political occasion, a facts story commenced out circulating on Twitter, claiming a scandalous revelation about one of the applicants. The tweet were given masses of retweets and caused an uproar.

Manipulation: The tale grew to emerge as out to be false, originating from a bot account with manipulated information and pics. By the time the truth have become out, the harm was finished, and public opinion become swayed.

Lesson: Always affirm news from real assets. Be careful of sensational tales, mainly for the duration of crucial occasions, and resist the urge to percentage unverified information.

four. Gaming Platform Betrayal

Background: Alex, 15, performed a web multiplayer pastime wherein he met "Jake." Over time, they've emerge as right buddies, sharing gaming strategies and private lifestyles testimonies.

Manipulation: Jake happy Alex to percentage his gaming credentials to get some different in-game gadgets. However, as quickly as Jake had get right of access to, he locked Alex out, stole his virtual assets, or maybe pressured him the usage of his very very own account.

Lesson: No be counted wide variety how near you revel in to online friends, in no way percentage private information or passwords. Keep gaming and real-lifestyles separate.

In each of those instances, the manipulators preyed on don't forget, emotion, or haste. Online, in which verifying authenticity is greater tough, it will become crucial to technique conditions and those with a mix of consider and skepticism.

Chapter 14: Emotional Abuse In Different Settings

Workplace Dynamics

The place of job is a microcosm of society, reflecting severa personalities and strength dynamics. Ideally, this environment promotes collaboration, innovation, and mutual recognize. Unfortunately, at instances, the place of business can also end up a breeding floor for emotional abuse, manifesting in diffused or overt methods.

Hierarchical Manipulation

In many agencies, hierarchy plays a crucial role. While structure is crucial for order and responsibility, it can additionally be exploited. Superiors may also moreover use their positions to belittle, intimidate, or undermine subordinates. This abuse can take the shape of public humiliation, regular criticism with out optimistic feedback, or placing unrealistic expectancies to set personnel up for failure.

The Toxic Co-employee

While plenty reputation is positioned on supervisor-employee dynamics, peers also can be perpetrators of emotional abuse. The toxic co-worker might also moreover unfold rumors, ostracize a colleague, or continuously take credit score score rating for some other's artwork. Their processes are regularly diffused, making them greater hard to pinpoint and deal with.

Subtle Signs within the Workplace

Overly important emails with a cc to superiors, intending to disgrace as opposed to provide comments.

Consistent exclusion from conferences or social sports, essential to expert and social isolation.

Unwarranted monitoring or thinking, growing an ecosystem of mistrust and anxiety.

Consequences of Workplace Emotional Abuse

The implications of such abuse are multi-fold. Victims regularly enjoy decreased assignment satisfaction, lower productivity, and a decline in mental health. It's now not unusual for them to expand tension or depressive troubles. Additionally, the business enterprise as an entire can also be affected by the usage of better turnover costs, reduced morale, and a tainted reputation.

Addressing the Issue

Combatting emotional abuse in the place of business calls for a collective attempt:

1. Open Communication: Encouraging open communicate wherein personnel can percent their issues without fear of retribution.

2. Clear Policies: Implementing and upholding strict regulations in competition to any form of abuse, ensuring that perpetrators face outcomes.

3. Support Systems: Creating help mechanisms like counseling offerings or helplines for affected employees.

4. Promote Positive Culture: Fostering a bit life-style that values mutual understand, facts, and teamwork.

In stop, the place of work, like every other setting, has its set of demanding situations. Recognizing and addressing emotional abuse is important for the well-being of employees and the general fulfillment of the company. It's now not pretty a lot commercial company productiveness; it is approximately safeguarding the intellectual and emotional fitness of folks who devote a extraordinary element in their lives to their jobs.

Friendships and Familial Relationships

Emotional abuse is not restrained to romantic relationships or place of business settings. Often, it insidiously weaves itself into the very bonds we hold costly: friendships and familial ties. These relationships, built on receive as proper with, statistics, and intimacy, can now and again be the toughest places to apprehend and address such abuse because of their deeply non-public nature.

The Dynamics in Friendships

Friendships are built on mutual be given as true with, respect, and affection. Yet, they may be marred by means of way of imbalances and exploitations:

1. One-sided Relationships: When one celebration commonly offers—emotionally, financially, or in terms of time—and the alternative continuously takes with out reciprocation, it could be a purple flag.

2. Belittling: Constantly putting down one's achievements, aspirations, or lifestyles choices below the guise of 'joking' or 'being honest.'

3. Emotional Blackmail: Using guilt or emotional misery to manipulate options or get one's way in conditions.

Familial Ties: A Complex Web

Familial relationships are inherently complex due to the depth of shared records and the variety of emotions worried.

1. Overbearing Control: Especially regular in decide-toddler dynamics in which, even in maturity, one's selections, manner of existence, or partners are excessively controlled or critiqued.

2. Scapegoating: Consistently blaming a particular family member for troubles, no matter the real motive.

3. Silent Treatment: Employing prolonged periods of non-communique as punishment or manipulation.

Subtle Signs in Friendships and Families

Constantly evaluating to others, essential to feelings of inadequacy.

Creating an environment of 'strolling on eggshells', in which expressing critiques will become a deliver of anxiety.

Trivializing concerns, feelings, or studies.

Consequences of Emotional Abuse in Personal Relationships

The scars left behind through emotional abuse in friendships and circle of relatives may be deep and lasting. It impacts arrogance, accept as authentic with in relationships, and may result in prolonged durations of isolation, melancholy, or anxiety.

Breaking the Cycle

1. Set Boundaries: Clearly defining what behaviors are unacceptable and sticking to results at the same time as the ones obstacles are violated.

2. Seek Counseling: Professional guidance can provide coping strategies, specially in entangled familial conditions.

3. Open Dialogue: Foster an surroundings wherein problems may be voiced with out fear.

four. Reevaluate Relationships: Not all relationships are well well worth saving. Sometimes, for one's nicely-being, it is probably critical to distance oneself or sever ties.

5. Build a Support System: Surrounding oneself with effective, supportive individuals can be a counterbalance to the negativity.

In end, friendships and familial relationships shape the bedrock of our social lifestyles. Recognizing and addressing emotional abuse inner those bonds is crucial. Everyone deserves recognize, information, and proper affection of their closest relationships.

Romantic Relationships and Dating

Romantic relationships maintain a unique vicinity in our lives. They are in which we're searching out mutual love, knowledge, companionship, and, often, a future collectively. The pleasure, vulnerability, and intimacy that constitute those relationships also make them functionality grounds for emotional abuse.

Early Days: The Dating Phase

The early degrees of a dating, in which people are absolutely mastering every specific, can set the tone for what follows:

1. Love Bombing: An overwhelming show of love and hobby initially, this is used later as leverage or withdrawn suddenly as punishment.

2. Testing Boundaries: Subtly pushing limits to look what you may be capable of get away with, along side invasive questions or actions that disrespect personal barriers.

three. Red Flags: Statements that belittle or degrade, no matter the truth that furnished humorously; excessive jealousy or tries to isolate you from pals and circle of relatives.

Deeper Commitment: Evolving Dynamics

As relationships evolve and develop deeper, so can the complexity of emotional manipulation:

1. Gaslighting: Making the partner doubt their notion, reminiscence, or emotions through denying or changing beyond events and conversations.

2. Control and Jealousy: Excessive manipulate over a associate's sports, social interactions, or possibly economic assets, regularly under the guise of hassle.

3. Emotional Withdrawal: Intentionally becoming far flung or withholding affection to gain leverage or as a form of punishment.

Signs of Emotional Abuse in Romantic Relationships

Chapter 15: Interactive Tools And Techniques

In the adventure of understanding, navigating, and restoration from emotional abuse, interactive system can function brilliant aids. Worksheets for self-reflected image, specially, provide a installed way to delve into private opinions, triggers, vulnerabilities, and strengths. They facilitate a guided introspection, which may be instrumental in restoration and constructing resilience.

Worksheets for Self-mirrored image: Why They Matter

Self-mirrored image, at the equal time as guided ard based, can help within the following techniques:

1. Clarify Feelings and Emotions: Putting thoughts and feelings down on paper should purpose them to clearer and further tangible.

2. Track Patterns: Over time, revisiting the ones worksheets can help people

apprehend habitual patterns in behavior, triggers, or responses.

3. Set Goals: They may be a platform to set restoration or non-public increase dreams and track development within the route of them.

4. Facilitate Communication: For the ones seeing a therapist or counselor, the ones worksheets can help articulate emotions and studies extra correctly.

Sample Worksheets:

1. Emotional Inventory: A worksheet to listing down emotions felt over each week or month, the triggers, and the subsequent reactions. This aids in expertise one's emotional panorama.

2. Boundary Setting: An workout to outline what is quality and what's no longer in interpersonal relationships, assisting establish and assert non-public barriers.

three. Self-actually actually well worth Affirmations: A area to put in writing superb affirmations that resource self confidence, which can be revisited in moments of doubt or distress.

4. Relationship Red Flags: Reflect on beyond relationships or interactions, discover capability red flags or moments wherein non-public barriers had been breached, and strategize a manner to cope with them inside the future.

five. Coping Strategies Log: List down situations that felt overwhelming and the coping mechanisms hired. This can assist refine strategies that artwork and discard folks who don't.

6. Gratitude Journal: A simple but effective tool, specializing in exceptional factors and things to be thrilled about, thereby instilling a sense of want and positivity.

Making the Most of these Worksheets:

1.   Consistency is Key: Regularly filling out these worksheets can offer the most accurate insights into one's emotional adventure.

2.   Honesty: For those tool to be powerful, absolute honesty with oneself is vital.

3.   Safe Storage: Due to the private and sensitive nature of the facts, make certain those worksheets are stored in a stable region.

4.   Review and Reflect: Periodically evaluation beyond entries to gauge improvement, understand patterns, and adapt strategies.

Interactive equipment and strategies, in particular worksheets for self-mirrored photo, provide a beneficial beneficial resource in the journey to understand and heal from emotional abuse. When used successfully, they'll be the catalyst for profound private growth and transformation.

Quizzes to Identify Toxic Traits or Situations

Quizzes can be powerful equipment for self-interest. They can assist individuals pinpoint complex behaviors, every in themselves and in others, that may not be brazenly identified. Presented underneath is a set up quiz aimed toward supporting you come to be aware of toxic tendencies or situations. This quiz, even as whole, isn't exhaustive. It's important to interpret consequences as a guiding principle and not a strict evaluation.

QUIZ: Recognizing Toxic Traits & Situations

Instructions: For every statement, pick out the choice that notable fits your feelings or reviews. Remember, there aren't any proper or wrong solutions; it's approximately your reality.

1. Relationship Dynamics

a. People frequently inform me that I'm too sensitive or that I overreact.

Rarely

Sometimes

Often

Always

b. I feel like my opinions or feelings are regularly left out or belittled.

Rarely

Sometimes

Often

Always

2. Self-Perception

a. I doubt my emotions or reminiscences approximately fine conditions, wondering I is probably remembering them wrong.

Rarely

Sometimes

Often

Always

b. I discover myself making excuses for someone else's conduct within the course of me.

Rarely

Sometimes

Often

Always

three. Communication Patterns

a. Conversations with sure humans depart me feeling harassed or like I'm the handiest guilty.

Rarely

Sometimes

Often

Always

b. I regularly sense like I'm walking on eggshells, on the lookout for to keep away from struggle.

Rarely

Sometimes

Often

Always

four. Emotional Well-being

a. I regularly enjoy tired or emotionally exhausted after interacting with unique humans.

Rarely

Sometimes

Often

Always

b. I locate it difficult to unique my emotions or issues out of worry of retaliation or mockery.

Rarely

Sometimes

Often

Always

Scoring:

Rarely: 1 element

Sometimes: 2 factors

Often: three factors

Always: 4 factors

Interpretation:

eight-16 Points: Your relationships appear to have a great basis of understand and conversation. However, it's normally beneficial to stay vigilant and address any issues inside the event that they get up.

17-24 Points: There can be a few minor crimson flags on your relationships. It's an notable idea to mirror on precise interactions or patterns that might be causing misery.

25-32 Points: The quiz indicates some strong symptoms and signs and symptoms and symptoms and symptoms of toxic dynamics. Consider looking for recommendation, remedy, or counseling to delve deeper into the ones patterns.

This quiz is designed to provide insights but need to not replace expert judgment. If you have got have been given issues about your relationships, keep in mind looking for expert advice.

In end, quizzes like the ones can be powerful in losing mild on regions of state of affairs inside interpersonal dynamics. By figuring out those early on, one ought to take steps towards greater healthy relationships and advanced emotional nicely-being.

Steps to Create a Personal Action Plan

Creating a private movement plan is akin to placing a roadmap in your journey within the direction of restoration, self-improvement, or accomplishing unique dreams. It offers clarity at the "where," "why," and "how" of your desires. Let's smash down the steps to create a complete and powerful personal movement plan.

1. Define Clear Objectives:

Start by using way of identifying what you desire to gain on the side of your movement plan. Whether it is recovery from emotional trauma, improving verbal exchange abilties, or placing limitations, your goal need to be smooth and particular.

Consider using the S.M.A.R.T (Specific, Measurable, Achievable, Relevant, Time-positive) criterion to outline your dreams.

2. Self-Assessment:

Before you chart a path ahead, recognize in which you currently stand. This includes recognizing your strengths, weaknesses, opportunities, and threats (SWOT assessment).

Reflect on beyond stories: What techniques worked for you? What demanding situations did you face?

three. Prioritize Your Goals:

If you've got multiple goals, rank them primarily based on urgency or importance.

It's often useful to cope with greater honest goals first, as achieving them can offer you with the self assure to cope with greater complex problems.

four. Break Down Tasks:

Divide your primary targets into smaller, capability responsibilities. This makes the approach plenty less overwhelming and gives a clearer route to progress.

Assign a timeline to each venture, making sure you have sensible expectations.

five. Identify Resources and Support:

List down gadget, assets, or humans that might assist you in reaching your obligations. This may encompass books, treatment, help organizations, or relied on friends.

Chapter 16: Creating Boundaries And Safe Spaces

Defining Personal Boundaries

Boundaries are the personal limits we set for ourselves in relationships, dictating how we permit others to cope with us and what behaviors we're capable of and might not tolerate. They are critical for preserving our self confidence, emotional safety, and common properly-being. A existence without boundaries can often lead to feelings of being used, taken as a proper, or perhaps abused.

Personal boundaries can be physical, emotional, or highbrow. Physical limitations would possibly involve your non-public area, your body, or your assets. Emotional and highbrow obstacles, but, can incorporate your emotions, thoughts, or non-public values.

To define your personal limitations:

1. Understand Your Values: Recognizing what you stand for is pivotal. What are your core beliefs? What values do you preserve

near? Knowing those can act as a manual whilst placing obstacles.

2. Listen to Your Feelings: If a few trouble does now not enjoy proper, it's miles generally a signal that a boundary has been crossed. Trust your instincts and feelings; they may be frequently your first alert device.

3. Communicate Clearly: It's now not sufficient genuinely to recognize your barriers; you need to specific them. Use clear, direct language.

four. Avoid Apologies: Remember, it is good enough to have limitations. You do not need to make an apology for looking after your well-being.

5. Be Consistent: Once you've got set a boundary, stick to it. Consistency reinforces your determination in your well-being.

6. Practice Self-recognition: Be sincere with yourself. Sometimes, the hardest obstacles are those we need to set with ourselves. Are you overextending? Are you

sacrificing your values for a person else's gain?

7. Seek Support: If you battle with setting or retaining imitations, trying to find steerage. This should come from relied on buddies, circle of relatives, or experts.

Creating consistent areas and boundaries is an ongoing way. As you grow, evolve, and trade, your limitations might probable shift, and that is adequate. The crucial component is ensuring you constantly prioritize your well-being and emotional health.

Practical Steps to Enforce Personal Boundaries

Establishing obstacles is first-rate the first step. Ensuring they may be legitimate and maintained is equally, if no longer greater, important. These realistic steps can manual you in enforcing your private barriers efficaciously:

1. Clear Communication: Begin with the aid of honestly mentioning your boundaries.

Whether it is a desire on communication channels, time availability, or emotional topics, be direct and concise.

2. Stay Calm and Collected: Even even as someone demanding situations or disrespects your obstacles, stay calm. Respond with composure in region of reacting all of a sudden.

three. Reinforce Your Boundaries: If a person maintains to brush aside your limitations, remind them gently however firmly. If a coworker continuously interrupts your lunch damage with work matters, reiterate: "I take this time to recharge, are we able to talk this as quickly as I'm decrease once more at my desk?"

four. Limit Exposure: If a person continuously violates your obstacles, endure in mind restricting your interaction with them. This can also endorse converting exercises, putting particular verbal exchange tips, or seeking out mediation.

five. Follow Through on Consequences: If a boundary is crossed, be prepared to comply with through with any previously mentioned outcomes. If you have got stated that you will give up a verbal exchange if a selected situation rely arises and it does, evenly exit the verbal exchange.

6. Practice Self-reflected image: Sometimes, the purpose a boundary is constantly crossed is that it is not clear or practical. Periodically re-compare and modify your obstacles if crucial.

7. Seek Support: Share your limitations with a near friend or member of the family who can help keep you accountable and offer encouragement while enforcing gets difficult.

eight. Model Respectful Behavior: By respecting the boundaries of others, you model the behavior you choice to look, making it more likely others will recognize your barriers in return.

nine. Reevaluate and Adjust: As you develop and evolve, your boundaries might also need to trade. Regularly don't forget whether your obstacles align with your contemporary dreams and values and alter as crucial.

Remember, limitations aren't approximately controlling others but rather approximately setting up what you can and couldn't gather. By following the ones practical steps, you empower yourself to stay in alignment collectively with your values and dreams, fostering greater healthy, extra respectful relationships.

Reclaiming Personal Power

Reclaiming personal energy is ready regaining manage over one's lifestyles, feelings, and selections. It's a adventure of self-discovery, resilience, and empowerment, particularly after experiencing situations in which one felt powerless or marginalized. Here's the way to undertake this transformative journey:

1. Acknowledge Past Powerlessness: Accept and recognize moments even as you felt disempowered. It's vital to confront the ones emotions head-on, records that they do not outline you, but are part of your information.

2. Affirm Your Worth: Regularly remind your self of your certainly nicely really worth. Use excessive excellent affirmations, journaling, or perhaps meditation to enhance your value and talents.

3. Set Clear Boundaries: As noted formerly, defining and enforcing personal limitations is pivotal. They act as safeguards, making sure you're dealt with with the honour you deserve.

4. Seek Knowledge: Empowerment regularly comes from information. Whether it's far learning approximately emotional intelligence, looking for recovery insights, or clearly gaining more records in a professional area, training can growth your self guarantee and experience of authority.

five.   Practice Assertiveness: Instead of being passive or overly aggressive, reason for assertiveness. Express your needs, feelings, and critiques respectfully and clearly.

6.   Listen to Your Inner Voice: Trust your instincts. More frequently than no longer, your intestine feeling will manual you closer to options that align on the facet of your private power.

7.   Engage in Empowering Activities: Take up sports activities that make you feel sturdy and prepared. This may be physical carrying occasions like martial arts or yoga, or intellectual carrying occasions like puzzle-solving, reading, or undertaking stimulating debates.

www.ingramcontent.com/pod-product-compliance
Lightning Source LLC
Chambersburg PA
CBHW071439080526
44587CB00014B/1911